YORK NOTES

LIBRARY AND LEARNING RESOURCES CENTRE
Northern College, Barnsley.   S75 3ET

Please return this book by the last date stamped below

 Longman      York Press

The right of Sarah Darragh to be identified as Author of this
Work has been asserted by them in accordance with the
Copyright, Designs and Patents Act 1988

YORK PRESS
322 Old Brompton Road, London SW5 9JH

PEARSON EDUCATION LIMITED
Edinburgh Gate, Harlow,
Essex CM20 2JE, United Kingdom
Associated companies, branches and representatives throughout the world

First published 1999
This new and fully revised edition first published 2005
Sixth impression 2009

ISBN: 978-1-4058-0172-0

Typeset by Pantek Arts Ltd, Maidstone, Kent
Produced by Pearson Education Asia Limited, Hong Kong

CONTENTS

PART ONE

INTRODUCTION

HOW TO STUDY A NOVEL

Studying a novel on your own requires self-discipline and a carefully thought-out work plan in order to be effective.

- You will need to read the novel more than once. Start by reading it quickly for pleasure, then read it slowly and thoroughly.

- On your second reading make detailed notes on the plot, characters and themes of the novel. Further readings will generate new ideas and help you to memorise the details of the story.

- Some of the characters will develop as the plot unfolds. How do your responses towards them change during the course of the novel?

- Think about how the novel is narrated. From whose point of view are events described?

- A novel may or may not present events chronologically: the time-scheme may be a key to its structure and organisation.

- What part do the settings play in the novel?

- Are words, images or incidents repeated so as to give the work a pattern? Do such patterns help you to understand the novel's themes?

- Identify what styles of language are used in the novel.

- What is the effect of the novel's ending? Is the action completed and closed, or left incomplete and open?

- Does the novel present a moral and just world?

- Cite exact sources for all quotations, whether from the text itself or from critical commentaries. Wherever possible find your own examples from the novel to back up your opinions.

- Always express your ideas in your own words.

These York Notes offer an introduction to *Emma* and cannot substitute for close reading of the text and the study of secondary sources.

CHECK THE BOOK

The York Handbook Dictionary of Literary Terms, by Martin Gray, provides explanations of the special vocabulary that will help you understand and write about novels like *Emma*.

READING *EMMA*

Jane Austen writes about love, desire, money and social politics. It is no wonder that film and period drama makers enjoy continued success with her novels As love stories, they never fail to provide the sense of romantic justice and calm moral balance which restores order to the world and composure to the heart. And of course, there is the delightful addition of deft social **satire** and calculated humour.. Her six novels, too, retain a commanding presence in the English literary heritage. As observational documentaries, they provide a highly concentrated source of socio-historical information about life in early-nineteenth-century England.

Austen wrote *Emma* in 1814. It was her penultimate novel, published (in 1816) one year before her death. Her work has been both criticised for the small world it encompasses, and vaulted for its accurate depiction of life in wealthy Home Counties England. Austen's success, however, stems from her awareness that the greatest novelists write about what they know. By focusing her writing on her own geographical area and social circle, her attention to detail was absorbed in the creation of character; living, breathing characters who inhabit the novels with an incomparable depth and individuality.

'I am going to take a heroine whom no one but myself will like,' said Jane Austen of her most dazzling of central characters, Emma Woodhouse. In spite of her creator's apparent caution as to the possibility of emotional engagement with a central character as lacking in internal wisdom and depth of character, Emma has found and retained an affectionate place in the hearts and minds of readers for over two centuries. Her youthful impetuosity and misguided attempts to shape and control the lives of others is observed through the watchful, bitingly honest but inevitably benevolent eyes of an **omniscient narrator**. Almost like the process of watching one's child learn and grow by its mistakes, the reader is invited to observe Emma's growth into self-knowledge and maturity through a series of blunders and miscalculations.

CHECK THE FILM

Check the film: There are several film versions of *Emma*, each with its own merits. Watchable versions include the 1996 version directed by Douglas McGrath starring Gwyneth Paltrow and the 1997 version directed by Dairmund Lawrence. For a modern take on the story, *Clueless* (1995) starring Alicia Silversone is an entertaining film.

Emma's comfortable financial status marks her as different to Austen's other heroines. 'Handsome, clever and rich' (Ch. 1, p. 5), with high social standing in her community, dominance in her household, and apparent complete emotional contentment, she is freed from the constraints of her contemporaries; she does not have to view marriage as a means to social and financial security. She asserts satisfaction with her life with serenity and has no interest in the romantic or financial benefits of wedlock. However, her preoccupation with matters of the heart, albeit not her own, marks her as a romantic. Her interference in the lives of others, particularly her friend Harriet Smith, stems from concern over the emotional happiness of her friends. The reader is left waiting for the inevitable meeting of the hearts between Emma and her friend and neighbour, the honourable and decent Mr Knightley. He waits for Emma to reach emotional maturity, ever the watchful friend, the harshest critic and Emma's voice of reason. When her natural intelligence and wit is finally focused upon herself through a delightful sense of **poetic justice**, the novel may reach its happy conclusion; the equal marriage of minds.

Emma is a romantic novel as well as a novel of the **Romantic** period.

It is a love story in the true sense of the word 'romantic', but is also concerned with emotional freedom and intensity. Austen's work is never more concerned with the social mores of marriage than in *Emma*, where contented matches are made within the strict social codes of society, thus satisfying the undeniably intense need for social status to be maintained. Emma's social circle are the 'middle class' – Emma has aspirations towards landed gentry and the depth of her snobbery pokes fun at the insecure social standing of this relatively new strand of the class structure. Austen's observational stance of social **realist** allows for discussion of whether conforming to social dictates can ever allow for complete emotional satisfaction. By exploring the possibilities of rebellion rather than blandly asserting the correctness of such a path through elegant wit and ironic detachment, she advocates independence of thought and decision and permits the reader to decide for themselves.

CHECK THE NET

Use a comprehensive online encyclopedia such as http://en.wikipedia.org for lists of authors, descriptions and detailed information on 'Romanticism'.

PART TWO

THE TEXT

NOTES ON THE TEXT

Emma was begun on 21 January 1814 and finished on 29 March 1815, It was published in three volumes in 1816 by John Murray of London. Two thousand copies were printed, of which 1,250 were sold within the year. The second edition appeared in 1833, and the novel was frequently reprinted during the nineteenth century, with an illustrated edition in 1896. One great edition of *Emma* is in the Oxford University Press series of the novels of Jane Austen, edited, with notes and appendices by R.W. Chapman, Oxford University Press, Oxford, 1923; reprinted at least twelve times. *Emma* has also appeared in the Oxford English Novels series, edited by David Lodge, Oxford University Press, 1971. Although the last two are both one-volume editions, they keep to the three-volume scheme, with chapter numbers and pagination corresponding to those of the original three volumes.

The text used in these Notes is the Penguin Popular Classics edition (1994). Here the chapter numbers are sequential, in one volume. The Penguin edition's Chapters 1–18 correspond to Volume I of the three-volume edition; Chapters 19–36 to Volume II, and Chapters 37–55 to Volume III.

SYNOPSIS

Emma Woodhouse is almost twenty-one years of age at the beginning of the novel; a significant age, as twenty-one was the age of adult independence in the eyes of the law and of society in eighteenth- and nineteenth-century England.

That she is not quite 'of age' is significant, as the novel concentrates largely upon Emma's journey into adult consciousness and maturity. At twenty-one, one was considered experienced and mature enough to make reasoned decisions about marriage, finances, friendships and the future; in other words, old enough to take control of your life and lead it purposefully. To all intents and

CONTEXT

Until the age of twenty-one, your position and status in society was that of a child, and you could do nothing without the proven permission of a parent/guardian.

purposes, Emma has had a great deal of control of her life from a very early age. She is the younger daughter of Mr Woodhouse of Hartfield in the village of Highbury in Surrey. Her older sister Isabella is married to Mr John Knightley and lives with her family in London, some sixteen miles away. Their mother died in Emma's infancy; therefore she has had little parental guidance other than that of her much older father. He, being 'valetudinarian' (Ch. 1, p. 6) in his approach and attitude to life, is fearful of change and disruption of any kind; very quiet in his habits and older than his years in his ways. Emma's beloved governess Miss Taylor has recently married a local gentleman by the name of Weston. At the opening of the novel both Emma and Mr Woodhouse are keenly aware of the change in their lifestyle and domestic routines engendered by the absence of 'poor Miss Taylor' (Ch. 2, p. 15). Emma's consolation in her loss stems from self-congratulation in engineering the match between the newly-weds – in spite of protestations to the contrary from George Knightley, John's brother and a loyal family friend. He points out to her that simply wishing for a romance to take place does not entitle her to claim the credit for the wedding. This first exchange between them shows him to be a man of sense, experience and sensitivity; blunt but kind, honest and fair with a deep attachment to Emma and her family whilst retaining a sensibility to her faults and an earnest desire to have them remedied. He demonstrates here his ability to see Emma for who she is; the only person in her acquaintance who is not blindly infatuated by her.

Notwithstanding Knightley's comments, Emma's quick mind and satisfaction with herself as a matchmaker soon make her cast her eyes around again for a new project to fill her time. She lights upon a pupil at the local school, a young woman by the name of Harriet Smith; a pretty, simple girl with gentle manners but also the social inconvenience of 'undisclosed' parentage.

Emma designs to make a friend of her and soon the young Harriet is a regular visitor and companion to Emma at Hartfield. This causes consternation to Mr Knightley; he disapproves of the friendship between them, feeling it will bring nothing good to neither party. In spite of his objections however, the friendship flourishes and Emma is soon rewarded in her search for a new romantic match to be made.

CONTEXT

Illegitimacy was an enormous social slur in the nineteenth century; Harriet's natural father has placed her anonymously in school in order to remove any social stigma from either himself or his daughter.

The local vicar, a Mr Elton, is another frequent visitor at Hartfield. Emma convinces herself that he would be an excellent prospect for Harriet; once convinced, she wastes no time in planting the seed of the idea in the mind of her friend. Harriet is so easily influenced by Emma's opinion that she rejects a proposal of marriage from an eminently more suitable admirer Robert Martin, a local farmer and friend of Mr Knightley (much to that gentleman's annoyance). Both girls continue in their idea that Mr Elton is not only enamoured of Harriet but means to make her an offer of marriage. It is during this first volume of the novel that the objective narrative stance contains much **dramatic irony**. The reader is allowed to witness Mr Elton's increasing attachment to Emma with mounting pleasure whilst she remains blissfully unaware of his infatuation and continues to misconstrue every sign of affection to herself as further indication of his affection for Harriet. Elton is far from a romantic fool however; whilst not insensible to the merits of beauty and sweetness in a woman, he values the worth of a high-born position in society as well as wealth, as Emma is warned by Mr Knightley.

CONTEXT

Mr Elton, although a son of a 'gentleman', would be perceived by Emma, as the heiress to landed gentry, as beneath her in the strict lines of social standing.

The drama reaches its crisis at Christmas. Isabella and her family have come to stay and the whole party are invited by the Westons for dinner. Harriet is taken ill with a severe cold and is unable to attend, and Emma is surprised and displeased by Mr Elton's apparent ability to enjoy himself despite the indisposition of the love of his life. She takes no heed of the warning from her brother-in-law that Mr Elton appears to be remarkably attached to herself rather than her friend, and persists in her fiction: until the pair are driven home together in the Woodhouse carriage. Trapped together like this, Elton wastes no time in declaring himself most volubly to Emma. Dismayed and insulted, she firmly puts him in his place and he retreats into a sullen silence after bluntly asserting his purpose to make a marriage of high social standing.

He shortly writes to her father, informing him that he intends to pay a visit to friends in a neighbouring county and will not return to Highbury for some weeks. When he does return, it is with a bride; a pushy, ill-bred but financially comfortable woman to whom he has presumably attached himself for financial gain.

Emma's consternation at her mistake is heartfelt and genuine. Her first and foremost thought is for the feelings of Harriet, and is highly sensible to her own guilt in encouraging an attachment. She is keenly aware, with the benefit of hindsight, of how she has misread Elton's signals and encouraged Harriet to fall completely in love with the man. Her admission of having 'blundered most dreadfully' (Ch. 16, p. 106), allows the reader to judge her less harshly than we might otherwise be tempted to do. Emma resolves to play no further part in the romantic affairs of others, and focuses all her attention in making amends to Harriet.

However, Volume 1 (Chapters 1–18) of the novel introduces the name of Mr Frank Churchill, the only son of Mr Weston from a previous marriage. At present he is a shadowy figure, known only by name and letter to the residents of Highbury who have a keen interest in the gentleman and a strong desire to meet him. Although the Westons have been married for some months, he has not yet paid a visit – something which arouses disapproval amongst the friends of Mrs Weston, and amongst Emma and Mr Knightley in particular. Emma has retained some fancy regarding Frank Churchill, as have the Westons; similar to her in age, situation and friends, she regards them as having a great deal in common and someone she may consider romantically herself.

In Volume II (Chapters 19–36), Frank Churchill eventually arrives to pay his long-awaited visit. Highbury has another visitor; Jane Fairfax, the niece of Mrs and Miss Bates; local residents and fond friends of Mr Woodhouse. Jane lives away from home, having been nominally adopted by a friend of her late father, Colonel Campbell and his wife.

Her visit is greeted with the same amount of pomp and circumstance as is that of Frank. Like Frank but for different reasons, Emma is often linked with Jane in the minds of their friends. Similar in years, education and accomplishments, the neighbourhood assume that they should be close companions for each other. However, and perhaps not surprisingly for a girl used to being the pivot and focus of so much kind attention, Emma is not as warmly attached to Jane Fairfax as others would assume her to be. In short, she is mindful that Jane's personality, looks and accomplishments threaten her position in the limelight.

CONTEXT
Frank's 'adoption' by Colonel Campbell does not mean the same as it would today. This family would financially sponsor rather than take over all familial roles of duty and care.

Frank proves to be everything the neighbourhood wished. Gallant, handsome and charming, he loses no time in delighting Emma and her friends with his kind words and pleasant manner. He is especially attentive towards Emma, and it is not long before she convinces herself that she is in love with him. She recognises quite quickly however that the warmth she feels towards him is nothing more than friendship; when he 'rescues' Harriet from an unpleasant encounter with a band of gypsies, Emma's match-making tendencies irresistibly join Frank and Harriet in her mind. Harriet admits that she is falling in love again and Emma, thinking she means Frank, encourages the attachment.

When Frank Churchill's guardian dies and releases him from familial dependence, the news of a secret engagement between Frank and Jane Fairfax is finally allowed to become clear, thus explaining both Frank's prolonged absence from, and return to, Highbury: he has wanted to retain proximity to Jane. Emma is concerned that her friend will be crushingly disappointed for the second time in months, and is very shocked that Harriet appears unconcerned at the news. She is horrified to find that she has unwittingly been encouraging her friend to fall in love with George Knightley. **Ironically** Emma, who could see no social imbalance in a marriage between Harriet and Mr Elton, or indeed Frank Churchill, finds the idea of union between Harriet and George Knightley to be preposterous and completely unacceptable. This dismay is her final indicator that she is in love with Knightley herself, but has convinced herself so completely of her own fiction regarding his feelings for Harriet that she holds out no hope for herself at all.

In consternation she sends Harriet away to stay with Isabella and John in London. George Knightley, who assumed that Emma was in love with Frank Churchill, visits to offer some comfort to her; when he discovers that he was mistaken in her attachment, he finally proposes to her himself. To complete the **closure**, Emma's new-found sense of humility hears with pleasure that Robert Martin repeated his proposal to Harriet in London and that, away from Emma's influence, she finally accepted him. Thus all romantic partnerships reach their satisfactory conclusion, and the novel ends with Emma reaching maturity in experience as well as age.

? QUESTION
Examine the ways in which Austen conveys the idea that a marriage between Mr Knightley and Emma will be part of a satisfying conclusion to the novel.

DETAILED SUMMARIES

CHAPTER 1

- We are introduced to Emma, her father and their circle.
- Emma is proud of being a matchmaker.

Emma and her father are sitting together at the close of a day of celebration – the wedding of Emma's beloved governess Miss Taylor to a friend and neighbour, Mr Weston. Mr Woodhouse is an elderly gentleman who seems older even than his years owing to a fearfulness of life and extreme preoccupation with health. In spite of the courteous authorial depiction of his 'gentle selfishness' (p. 7), he is clearly rather trying company and, in more unkind eyes, positively infuriating. Thus is a kinder aspect of Emma's character displayed; that she puts his comfort and mental well-being first, regardless of her own feelings, shows her to have the redeeming feature of kindness and concern for those whom she loves.

Emma is at pains to cheer her father from the sad loss of their friend, pointing out to him that Mrs Weston is delightfully settled in her new life and cannot want for anything. Mr Woodhouse, who finds it impossible to consider any other point of view but his own, cannot be persuaded that her departure is not a sad loss to all, including Emma.

Emma receives a welcome release from the prospect of a tedious and difficult evening when their friend Mr George Knightley pays a visit, clearly understanding the family well and sensitive to how they will be feeling this evening. Emma congratulates herself for her match-making capabilities bringing about the marriage between Miss Taylor and Mr Weston; he gently but bluntly points out to her that one cannot possibly take credit for a mere 'lucky guess' (p. 11). He admires endeavour and diligence, displaying sincere and warm regard for Emma coupled with an honest view of her, faults and all. He warns her that meddling in the affairs of others can bring nothing but trouble, but she refutes this roundly and in spite of his warnings, indicates her desire to find a partner for the local vicar, Mr Elton.

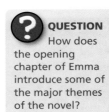

QUESTION
How does the opening chapter of Emma introduce some of the major themes of the novel?

COMMENTARY

The first chapter introduces us to the central character of the novel with its memorable summation of Emma's attributes and social standing; 'handsome, clever and rich, with a comfortable home and happy disposition' (p. 5). The opening section concentrates upon a detailed description of Emma's character and circumstances, therefore signalling her centrality within the novel. Inasmuch as introductory chapters have a deliberate function of focussing attention on important characters and themes, we are made conscious here that Emma's arrogance will play a vital role in the unfolding drama.

The preoccupation with marital status in this chapter also marks the significance of the theme to the novel as a whole. Emma's remarks upon Mr Elton's single status indicate that for this society, single life was seen as noticeably less desirable than marriage.

GLOSSARY

threatened alloy threatened to spoil

bride-people newly weds

valetudinarian a person constantly concerned with his own ailments

mizzle drizzle

chuse choose

CHAPTER 2

- We are given the history of Frank Churchill.

The narrator supplies interesting background information regarding the history of Mr Weston, his first marriage and his son, Frank Churchill. Mr Weston, or Captain Weston as he was then, married Miss Churchill of Enscome, much against the wishes of her older brother and his wife. Mrs Weston died after three years of marriage, and the son was given over to the charge of her family who undertook his upbringing and education. Mr Weston maintains regular contact with his son who is now grown up. Although they meet every year in London, Frank had never visited his father at his Highbury home of Randalls.

The neighbourhood expect that Frank Churchill show his respects to his father's new bride by paying a visit; he sends a congratulatory letter which is warmly received and discussed at length during social visiting.

COMMENTARY

Frank Churchill will play a significant role in the novel and it is important that his presence is introduced so early into the novel. The portrayal of his mother struggling to reconcile love over social circumstance will strike an interesting note for the reader later on; at present it highlights the theme of societal stratospheres being clearly demarked. Mr Weston's decision to marry a 'portionless' (p. 13) governess is clearly only allowed because as a mature man he can act as he pleases.

The narrator allows a moment of delightful ironic commentary when Mr Woodhouse frets over the neighbourhood eating the wedding cake; in spite of him paraphrasing Dr Perry's apparent concerns about its unwholesomeness, we are told of a 'strange rumour in Highbury of all the little Perry's being seen with a slice of Mrs Weston's wedding cake in their hands' (p. 16).

GLOSSARY

A small independence a small independent income

entering into the militia of his county, then embodied the militia was a branch of the military service, but not part of the regular army: it was drawn or 'marshalled' from local districts when required

an easy competence sufficient unearned income so as not to have to earn a living

portionless without a dowry

CHAPTER 3

- Emma meets Harriet Smith.

Emma looks forward to a dull evening at home. She has habitually invited some old friends of her fathers to supper; three ladies who often spend the evening at Hartfield. Mrs Bates and her maiden daughter are regular visitors, along with Mrs Goddard who runs the local girls boarding school. Emma evidently does not relish the prospect of spending the evening in such company, and as such is delighted when Mrs Goddard asks if she may be accompanied by one of her boarders. Harriet Smith, a very pretty girl of seventeen is described as 'the daughter of somebody' (p. 18). Emma has noticed her in Highbury before, principally because of her prettiness.

As the young women chat, plans form in Emma's mind of befriending Harriet and thus elevating her social status and improving her prospects. The idea of a project such as this cheers her spirits immensely and the evening flies past.

COMMENTARY

The reader is left in no doubt as to the conceit of which Emma is capable here. Harriet's principle endowments – other than her face – appear to be the flattering awe she holds Emma in, and which Emma so heartily commends as marks of good sense and judgement.

Harriet's illegitimacy is important. Social standing was predetermined by birth status and Emma's refusal to accept the importance of these rules causes her problems later on.

CHAPTER 4

- Emma objects to Harriet's 'unsuitable' romance

Once decided, Emma wastes no time in encouraging the friendship with Harriet, who is only too willing and compliant. Emma is honest in her reasoning; she needs a companion, she misses Mrs Weston, she can never repeat that kind of friendship but with Harriet will be able to do some good. She is aware that Harriet is very flattering company and in fact dotes on her every word, and is not insensible to the merits of that for her.

Harriet has a friendship with a local farming family by name of Martin; Emma questions her about this and soon suspects an attachment between the son, Robert Martin, and her friend. She is quick to discourage this, warning Harriet that the accident of her birth requires her to disassociate herself from any connections that would lower her status further. She is quick to use Mr Knightley as a model of propriety and gentlemanly bearing, thus showing the esteem in which she holds him herself.

COMMENTARY

The Martins appear to be an honest, decent family and Emma's objection to them – in comparison with her own circle – shows the snobbery and conceit of which she is capable. Harriet is of a lower class than herself, but she feels that the association with herself has raised the girl far beyond considerations of an alliance with a farming family.

CHAPTER 5

- Mr Knightley and Mrs Weston disagree about Emma and Harriet's friendship.

Mr Knightley and Mrs Weston discuss the friendship between Emma and Harriet. Mr Knightley is concerned that it may do harm to both, and certainly will bring nothing good. He is sensible to Emma's faults and knows that she will always take the path of least resistance rather than apply herself diligently to anything for her own improvement. He recalls a reading list she drew up at fourteen which showed a great deal of taste and sense, but which was never sustained. His concern stems from recognition that time spent with one inferior in education and sense does nothing to spur on desire for improvement.

They discuss Emma's future, musing over her resolution never to marry and wondering what will become of her. An allusion is made to Mr and Mrs Weston cherishing a secret hope in that direction, a hope which presumably involves romance with Frank Churchill.

COMMENTARY

Mr Knightley is shown to have a great deal of regard for Emma. He admires her physically; 'I love to look at her' (p. 31), he saved the reading list drawn up several years before, so impressed was he by the promise of effort and the marks of good taste in the content. His keen desire for her improvement and honest appraisal of her faults shows his good sense as well as his attachment.

> **GLOSSARY**
>
> **a subjection of the fancy to the understanding** she will never overcome her imagination with her intellect
>
> **wantonness of comfort** excessive comfort
>
> **out of conceit with** dissatisfied with
>
> **spleen** ill humour
>
> **this little remains of office** this small part left over from her position of governess

CHAPTER 6

- Emma paints a portrait of Harriet.

Emma's resolution to make a match between Mr Elton and Harriet gathers pace. The gentleman is a frequent visitor to Hartfield so there is plenty of opportunity for Emma to encourage feeling on both sides. She only needs to make the suggestion once to Harriet before the girl's simpleness, coupled with conviction of Miss

Chapter 6 continued

Woodhouse being right about everything, results in her convincing herself she is in love. As for Mr Elton, Emma feels that he has dropped enough hints and shown enough attentions to be at the point of making his declaration.

Emma decides to take up a long-discarded hobby of drawing. She determines that a portrait of Harriet would be a very good idea, and Mr Elton encourages this idea with alacrity. The portrait is painted, and Mr Elton carries it to London to be framed.

COMMENTARY

Both the narrator and Mr Knightley have commented on the 'misfortune' (Ch. 5, p. 29) for Emma of being used to having her own way. This chapter is full of irony: the reader benefits from the perspective created by authorial distance, and can see from the start that Mr Elton's attachment is to Emma herself. She prides herself on her judgement; momentary concern over the extent of the compliments he pays her is glossed over as proper attention to the friend of the beloved object.

The mixture of acuity and basic folly in her judgements is shown through her thoughts on Mr Elton; where she is rightly mindful of his sycophancy and slight want of gentility, she misses the point completely regarding the real object of his attentions.

Mr Knightley makes a straightforward observation on Emma's competency with portraiture; 'You have made her too tall, Emma' (p. 37). She privately agrees he is right; his judgement is rarely refuted although it may hurt.

GLOSSARY

Your likeness taken your portrait painted

I took him drew his portrait

cockade plume of hair on his head

declaration declaration of love leading to a proposal of marriage

complaisance desire to please

CHAPTER 7

- Harriet is proposed to – and refuses.

Harriet receives a letter containing a proposal of marriage from Robert Martin. Confused and agitated, she consults Emma over what she should do. Emma reads the letter and is surprised and impressed by the content and wording, but influences Harriet nevertheless to refuse the offer.

Harriet is clearly distressed by this proposition and remains unconvinced until Emma points out that their friendship would never be allowed to continue if Harriet was to marry Mr Martin. Once resolved, she writes a letter of refusal and Emma cheers her spirits by pondering over whether Mr Elton is presently showing her portrait around his friends and family in London.

COMMENTARY

The fact that Emma is surprised by the quality of Robert Martin's letter shows the extent of her pride and snobbery. Even Harriet, subservient to the last, jumps to his defence when Emma criticises him. At heart Harriet knows Emma is wrong but is so blinded by her superiority that she is left confused.

> **GLOSSARY**
> **I collect** I infer

CHAPTER 8

- Emma quarrels with Mr Knightley over Harriet's refusal of Robert Martin.

Subsequent to Harriet's refusal of Robert Martin, Mr Knightley pays Emma a visit. His uncommon praise of her is followed up with news that Robert Martin went to see him to solicit his advice over whether he should propose to Harriet. Although Mr Knightley had some concerns, Martin convinced him that he was so much in love that eventually he was persuaded. He tells Emma of his high regard for Martin and his family, and is assured of the man's good sense and judgement.

When Emma tells him that the proposal has arrived and been refused, Knightley is furious. He is quick to ascertain the part Emma has played in the refusal, and angrily remonstrates with her for bad judgement and self-seeking motives. He points out that Harriet could not make a better match than Robert Martin, and Emma filling her head with ideas of grandeur is nothing short of unkindness.

Although Emma is a worthy adversary, their quarrel upsets her. She values Mr Knightley's judgement and knows that he is not often wrong. Indeed, he has worked out that Emma has Mr Elton in mind for Harriet, and although she refutes this to his face, is made uneasy

> **GLOSSARY**
> **a most unexceptional quarter** a very pleasing source
> **settled provision** money legally settled upon her
> **canvassing** asking for support for
> **restoratives** pick-me-ups

Chapter 8 continued

nevertheless about his warning that Elton is determined to make a very good match and would certainly never look twice at Harriet Smith.

COMMENTARY

Austen clearly requires the reader to be aware of Mr Knightley's astute judgement. He is not wrong in his suspicions and his warnings will be made resonant later on in the novel.

CHAPTER 9

- Mr Elton's riddle misses its mark.

Emma and Harriet light on another means of filling their days; the collection and transcription of a series of riddles. They ask Mr Elton for help in their search and he obliges with one of his own; a riddle of love, a disguised declaration clearly written as a statement of intent for Emma. He leaves the riddle with them and they transcribe it into their book which he perceives as a sign of encouragement.

There is discussion of the proposed visit of Emma's sister Isabella, her husband and children for Christmas. Emma is very much looking forward to seeing her nieces and nephews.

COMMENTARY

The riddles provide a **metaphor** for the situation between Emma, Harriet and Mr Elton; an obvious answer to a puzzle waiting to be uncovered. **Ironically**, Emma is quick to work out the meaning of Elton's riddle in spite of being completely impervious to his feelings for her. The 'ready wit' (p. 56) he describes is an apt description of her, and highly inappropriate for Harriet, and yet even this is misinterpreted and ascribed to the blindness of love. Harriet on the other hand, agonises over the meaning and is still confused even when she has it explained to her.

GLOSSARY

a thin quarto of hot-pressed paper a slim 'book' which they have made by folding best-quality paper

in this age of literature, such collections on a very grand scale the narrator is being sarcastic; the riddles collected hardly constitute 'literature'

'Kitty, a fair but frozen maid' from a riddle by David Carrick, a well known actor (1717–79), published in the *New Foundling Hospital for Wit*, part IV (1771). It links Cupid (the god of love) and a chimney-sweep

My first doth affliction denote woe

Which my second is destined to feel man. The answer to the charade is 'wo(e)man', the best cure for that affliction

all *appropriation* all that makes the whole verse belong to one particular person (Emma thinks he means Harriet)

sure of his rubber sure of having enough people to play cards

effusion literary composition that is an outpouring of the author's feelings.

CHAPTER 10

- Emma gives her views of marriage.

Emma and Harriet pay a duty visit to tend to the needs of a local family who are very poor and have sickness at home. Emma brings food and medicine to them, and shows herself to be caring and capable in the face of practical need.

During discussion with Harriet, Emma states her decision never to marry. Harriet's concern over the social impoverishment of the status of old maid is roundly refuted by Emma's, who feels that she will have the best of all worlds without any of the concerns of the married woman.

The subject of Miss Bates' niece Jane Fairfax is broached, and Emma clearly and directly voices her irritation with the girl. Her distaste stems apparently from having to hear excessive praise of Jane whenever they are in the company of Miss Bates.

Mr Elton, who has been watching them from his window, hurries out and walks with them. Emma contrives to get an invitation into the Vicarage by breaking a shoelace and entreating the assistance of Mr Elton's housekeeper. This ruse works in the first instance, and Emma spends longer than necessary over her shoe repair in order to leave the pair alone together. However, the marriage proposal is still not forthcoming.

COMMENTARY

Emma's visit to the impoverished local family shows her compassion and warm-heartedness. She is generous, sensitive to their needs and keen to do all she can. This interlude allows for a display of her better qualities of sense, reason and good judgement.

Responsibility to those in one's neighbourhood in impoverished circumstances, was accepted by the higher-classes. Emma's visit is not unusual, and in fact would be expected as part of her duties.

GLOSSARY

pollards either trees that have had their tops removed; or sheep, cattle or deer with horns or antlers removed

the pattern of a stomacher instructions for making an ornamental bodice

half-boot a boot reaching to between the ankle and knee

Chapter 10 continued

However, she has a genuine concern and a sensible attitude to their plight; her act is selfless and displays a level of humility which would make Mr Knightley proud of her. The whole episode allows the reader to feel that she is not without hope of improvement.

CHAPTER 11

- The family arrive for Christmas.

Emma's sister and family arrive for their Christmas visit. Their arrival is greeted with great excitement as they have been absent at Hartfield for longer than normal.

The family discuss the change in situation of Mrs Weston, and Emma is at pains to assure Isabella that they see her almost as often as when she was living with them. Isabella is clearly as delicate and health-conscious as her father; apt to worry excessively over the most trifling matters. Her husband is painted as a blunter version of his brother, and Emma shows concern for the feelings of her father in worry over John Knightley's tendency towards insensitivity and rudeness. On this occasion however he is solicitude itself.

During discussion of Frank Churchill and his father giving over his care to the family of his dead wife, John Knightley makes some disparaging remarks about Mr Weston which Emma, although annoyed, chooses to ignore for the sake of peace.

COMMENTARY

Mr John Knightley is shown to be a gruffer version of his brother: the same good sense and practical mind, with family and home at the heart of his concerns. However, he has not the same sense of duty to others, or sensibility to the feelings of those around him. Emma is keenly aware of his tendency towards rudeness, and her ability to be sensible to this shows her own heightened sense of duty and care for the feelings of those she cares for.

GLOSSARY

Mr Knightley as the elder brother, he is not referred to by his first name George

any doubts of the air of Randalls any doubts as to whether or not the air there is healthy

Where is the young man? He means Frank Churchill

her brother frequently used where we would now say 'brother-in-law'

to look down on the common rate of social intercourse to despise the ordinary course of friendship and visiting outside his own home, which was 'all-sufficient' or enough for him

CHAPTER 12

- Emma and Mr Knightley make their peace – and keep the peace.

Mr Knightley is invited to dinner, against the wishes of Mr Woodhouse who selfishly wants to keep Isabella to himself. Emma's sense of right prevails in spite of being uncomfortable about the first contact since their quarrel. She devises a means of securing the best light for herself by having her baby niece on her lap when he arrives, thus softening the initial image of her in his eyes.

Although still concerned about her interference in the matter of Robert Martin's proposal to Harriet, Mr Knightley is as keen for the quarrel to be ended as Emma is herself. They make their peace with each other in spite of his reference to her as a 'spoiled child' (p. 77) and begging the advantage of years of experience.

After dinner, Isabella and her father engage on their favourite topic – health. Isabella matches her father's attachment to his own doctor Mr Perry with her Mr Wingfield in London, and the two absent apothecaries are soon made adversarial weapons in their respective advice to their patients. Emma is mindful to the sensitivity of such a subject, and takes repeated pains to steer the course of the conversation away from any possible disagreements. However, even she cannot anticipate in time Mr Woodhouse bemoaning the family's decision to take a holiday in South End; to the extent that John Knightley takes exception and becomes annoyed. His brother and Emma dextrously smooth over the atmosphere.

> **CONTEXT**
>
> Taking a trip to the coast in order to be revived by the sea air was becoming an increasingly popular pastime in the nineteenth century. Doctors prescribed a 'sea cure' often, believing that the cleaner air and salt water had healing properties.

COMMENTARY

Emma and Mr Knightley have a dual purpose which assists the cementing of their friendship. As allies in the cause of peace, they display similar qualities of sensitivity and understanding of others.

The sea air was thought to have healing properties and many travelled there for health reasons. Although Georgian society would be shocked at the idea of free swimming, they did bathe in the sea: for medicinal rather than recreational purposes.

CHAPTER 13

- Emma disapproves of Mr Elton's behaviour.

Mr and Mrs Weston have invited their closest friends for dinner on Christmas Eve. They party is very much looked forward to, even by Mr Woodhouse who rarely goes anywhere.

However, Harriet comes down with a severe cold and is too ill to attend. Emma visits her bedside and comforts her as much as she can. She is very surprised when she meets Mr Elton on the journey home and discovers that he still has every intention of going to the party in spite of the indisposition of his loved one.

Mr John Knightley, who meets Emma for her walk home, advises her that in his opinion, Mr Elton is paying her particular attention and that her actions appear to be encouraging him. Emma laughs off his recommendation that she take care and moderate her behaviour, believing as she does that he is completely mistaken.

John Knightley and Emma call for Mr Elton in their carriage on the way to the Westons. Mr Elton appears to be in remarkably high spirits, and Emma is astonished by his behaviour. His companionship is only marginally more agreeable than her brother-in-law's, who dislikes social occasions and bitterly resents leaving the warmth of the Hartfield fireside at Christmas.

GLOSSARY

Mr Elton's objects the object of this affections, that is, his beloved

that very day se'nnight that day week (se'nnight being seven nights)

COMMENTARY

Harriet's cold causes a great deal of consternation; the doctor is sent for and she is immediately bed-ridden. It has to be remembered that constitutions were far more delicate, medical advances in their infancy, infectious diseases rife, and mortality rates relatively high. Therefore all due care was being taken in this case as would be expected.

CHAPTER 14

- Mr Elton presses his attentions upon Emma.
- News arrives that Frank Churchill will shortly pay a visit to Highbury.

The guests arrive at Randalls and are warmly welcomed by their hosts. Emma continues to feel great concern over Mr Elton's cheerful mood. His attention to her is so intense that it crosses her mind that her brother-in-law may have been right; not in him being solely interested in herself, but in his affections having been transferred to her from Harriet. She is feeling very uncomfortable and is relieved to move away, at dinner, to sit next to Mr Weston.

He tells her the delightful news that his son Frank Churchill has written to say that he will be shortly able to pay his long-promised visit. His being released from Enscome depends entirely upon the caprice of his aunt, who is apparently known for her unpleasantness and unreasonable selfishness. Mrs Weston is less convinced of his arrival than her husband, but the news cheers Emma heartily. Like the Westons, she cherishes some secret wonder about the shadowy figure of Mr Churchill and is very much looking forward to meeting him.

COMMENTARY

Emma begins to prepare for a further disappointment, her imagination already having given her 'instinctive knowledge' (p. 94) of him, and that 'if she *were* to marry, he was the very person to suit her in age, character and condition' (p. 92).

> **CONTEXT**
>
> Emma's attitude to Frank Churchill is not as strangely unromantic as it may sound to a revisionist mind. Given that marriage at that time was more often than not a business partnership rather than a love match, Emma is in fact displaying pragmatism at the thought of an alliance between herself and Mr Churchill.

CHAPTER 15

- Mr Elton makes an unwelcome proposal.

In this chapter, the plot development of Volume 1 reaches its crisis. Mr John Knightley announces to Mr Woodhouse in a rather unfeeling manner that snow has begun to fall and is settling rapidly.

Mr Woodhouse is in a state of panic and the others struggle to calm down the agitation engendered by his son-in-law's callous announcement.

Mr Knightley and Emma discover that the snow is barely beginning to cover the ground and that if they leave straight away, they can travel the mile home by coach in complete safety. Amongst the commotion and solicitude for Mr Woodhouse, the pair speedily make the arrangements to leave.

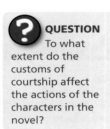

QUESTION
To what extent do the customs of courtship affect the actions of the characters in the novel?

To Emma's consternation, John Knightley gets into his wife's carriage for the journey home and she is left alone with Mr Elton. He immediately seizes her hand and protests his love for her, begging to be allowed her hand in marriage. Emma is shocked and dismayed by his apparent fickleness and initially assumes he is drunk; he protests that he never thought of Miss Smith in any way other than her friend, and that all his attentions have been made with the express purpose of courting herself. He believes himself to have been encouraged by Emma and insists that he would never have visited so frequently unless encouraged to do so. The conversation gets more heated as Mr Elton insists that he would never consider marrying at the 'level' (p. 102) of Harriet's social status. Emma bluntly and pointedly refuses his proposal, and an outraged silence ensues until the carriage reaches Mr Elton's door and he makes his escape.

When she returns home, her brother-in-law has regained his good temper and is anxious to make amends for his earlier rudeness. Emma is flustered and extremely disturbed by her encounter, but must pretend that all is well until she is alone.

COMMENTARY

Poor Emma's shock at hearing that not only has she been completely misguided but has unwittingly encouraged Mr Elton's erroneous assumption must be dreadful to bear, but there is comedy in the situation she finds herself and the reader cannot but feel that she deserves to feel uncomfortable. Mr Elton is not a sympathetic character and we feel little respect for his behaviour and views on social advancement; 'I need not so totally despair of an equal alliance, as to be addressing myself to Miss Smith!' (p. 102).

However, Emma has encouraged him through her own misguided and selfish attempts to form another romance, and has further been warned by both Knightley brothers. Her refusal to listen to that advice and her persistence in playing with the lives of others has caused this situation, and we cannot feel other than she is receiving her just deserts.

Her short exchange with Mr Knightley where they make the arrangements for the journey home is highlighted as the single portion of direct speech in that passage; visually demarking an island of speedy common sense and like-mindedness amongst confusion and fuss.

CHAPTER 16

- Emma makes her first blunder.

When finally alone, Emma's mind whirls at the effort of making sense of what has just happened. Her first thought is of the shock at finding out that all the attentions she supposed were for her friend, were in fact addressed to herself. This is followed by remembering what both Knightley brothers warned her, and an acquiescence to their 'penetration' (p. 104).

COMMENTARY

Emma is insulted by Mr Elton daring to hope that she would deign to consider him in marriage; highly insulted, she reminds herself that the Woodhouses are an ancient, long-established family with wealth far surpassing any the Elton's could lay claim to. She feels the affront that he would dare presume that she would sink so low as to consider him, and his estimation is further lowered in her mind for this.

She is, however, relatively clear about the part she has played in this mistake. She admits freely that she has encouraged him through action and word, and cannot blame him for misinterpreting her feelings when she did exactly the same herself.

Her final thought is for poor Harriet; she takes full blame for having talked her into love with Mr Elton and resolves to do

---

GLOSSARY

the sweep the curved carriage-drive leading to a house

her subject cut up her subject of conversation cut short

his half and half state she thinks he is half drunk and half sober everything in her power to put things right. She can do nothing immediately however as a heavy snowfall leaves everybody housebound for Christmas.

CHAPTER 17

- Mr Elton leaves for Bath, and Harriet is distraught.

The snow eventually clears and Isabella and John return home. Mr Woodhouse receives a short letter from Mr Elton, begging pardon for his sudden departure but announcing a visit to some friends in Bath. Emma is not addressed in the letter and she feels the deliberate slight but understands it.

She is relieved that Mr Elton will be out of the way for a few weeks; she can now not delay explaining to Harriet the reality of the situation.

Harriet is rightly devastated by the news which Emma delivers honestly and candidly, taking full blame for the mistake and the encouragement she gave her friend. She resolves to do everything in her power to make amends to Harriet for the pain she is suffering now.

COMMENTARY

Emma redeems herself in her determination to shoulder the blame and pay the consequences for her actions. She admires Harriet's simplicity and humility and, recognising the lack of such qualities in her own character, resolves to pay more attention to what her little friend can teach her.

CHAPTER 18

- Emma and Mr Knightley disagree – again.

Frank Churchill does not pay his visit, to the disappointment of everyone. Emma and Mr Knightley discuss his persistent absence and Emma finds herself somehow engaged in an argument with her friend whereby she is delivering the exact opposite to her true feelings.

Mr Knightley feels that Frank Churchill is extremely remiss in his lack of respect to the new status of his father, and that it is the whimsical selfishness of youth and pursuit of pleasure which keeps him away. Although Emma privately agrees with him, she argues that Frank cannot possibly go against the wishes of his demanding and overbearing aunt.

This is refuted by Mr Knightley who maintains that a grown man should have the strength of character to do what is morally and socially the right thing, regardless of any pressure he may be under. Emma comments on his determination to think badly of Frank before he has even met him and wonders what the root cause of this prejudice may be.

COMMENTARY

The placing of this conversation immediately prior to the start of Volume 2 indicates that Frank Churchill's presence will supersede the Elton drama in plot development, as indeed it does.

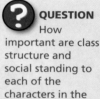

QUESTION
How important are class structure and social standing to each of the characters in the novel?

Emma and Mr Knightley appear to disagree often; Emma herself wonders at her rationale for perversely taking an opposing view to her real feelings, deliberately to engage him in verbal sparring.

Mr Knightley evidently values propriety and nobleness of character highly, and is suspicious of Frank's lack of duty to his father; Emma privately agrees. They both feel the slight on Mrs Weston's behalf and are concerned that he may not be worthy of the high praise he receives or the vaulted status he already has in Highbury society.

CHAPTER 19

- Miss Bates's chattering and news of Jane Fairfax annoys Emma.

Emma takes pains to comfort Harriet through her period of mourning over the loss of romantic promise to Mr Elton. Harriet's devotion is deep and remarkably resilient, and Emma has to muster every ounce of persistence in keeping her friend's mind away from thoughts of him.

The pair pay a visit to Mrs and Miss Bates, primarily as a distraction for Harriet but also because Emma knows she does not pay the ladies the attention she should, and has often been criticised by Mr Knightley and others for being remiss. She finds the visits wearing and tedious, largely due to Miss Bates' talkative manner and the preoccupation with the subject of her niece, Jane Fairfax. However, Emma judges that it is not the time for Jane to write so they should be safe from hearing one of her letters repeated over and over again.

She is wrong, however: they have received a letter that morning and Miss Bates spends so much time repeating the content of the letter that Emma and Harriet can make their escape without actually hearing the body of it read to them.

COMMENTARY

Chapter 19 marks the beginning of Volume II.

Emma is not alone in finding the rambling tongue of Miss Bates an irritation. Mrs Cole, another neighbour, apparently paid them a visit earlier in the day with the same hopes of being spared a letter from Jane Fairfax. Also, Miss Bates alludes to the fact that her mother finds her difficult to hear when she has no problems hearing Jane's – much quieter – voice. The narrator allows these points to pass without comment, allowing the reader to form their own conclusions.

Thus Emma is not being criticised for her severity of judgement; rather for her neglecting her duty in spite of personal feelings.

In spite of her resolve to never allow ideas of romantic fancy again, she cannot resist suspecting that Jane's decision to come to Highbury rather than pay a wedding visit to Mr and Mrs Dixon in Ireland has been influenced by a strong attachment between her and the groom.

GLOSSARY

beaufet buffet

my huswife a small case containing scissors, thread, needles and other sewing things

she fills the whole paper and crosses half finishes writing a page, turns it sideways and writes at right angles to what is already written – hence 'chequerwork', the criss cross effect

must make it very strange…countries after the Act of Union between Great Britain and Ireland in 1801, the two *countries* were part of the same *kingdom*

CHAPTER 20

- Jane Fairfax arrives.

Jane's history is opened to the reader. She is the orphaned daughter of Miss Bates' sister and Captain Fairfax, and was adopted by her father's superior, Colonel Campbell, upon the death of her parents. She has been brought up in their family as companion to their only daughter. Although the family are devoted to Jane, they cannot provide means for her independence, and it has always been understood that she would eventually take up a position as a governess.

Emma finds it difficult to like Jane. Mr Knightley observes that one possible, and very likely, reason is the pain of being faced with a young woman who is far more accomplished that she is herself. Jane has taken far more advantage of similar opportunities for self-improvement and is a better pianist, reader and artist than Emma will ever be. Her application and diligence can only show Emma in a bad light. Although Emma does not like this idea, she privately admits to its truth and resolves to be different.

The Bates' are invited to Hartfield for the evening and Emma does her best to change her feelings for Jane. However, time has made her forget the quiet reserve which always frustrated her in the past and she ends the evening more resolved than ever that she and Jane can never be friends. Jane has met Frank Churchill in Weymouth and Emma tries hard to find out more about him from her but is completely thwarted.

COMMENTARY

Jane Fairfax's situation was not uncommon to many young women in the eighteenth and nineteenth centuries. Women of a certain social class were not expected to earn their living, and indeed there were very few opportunities for women to work. If the family could not provide financial independence, a good marriage was one alternative. However, marriage was far more of a financial arrangement and if the young woman could offer nothing in the way of a dowry she had little hope of a good marriage.

GLOSSARY

camp-fever epidemics occurring in military camps, chiefly typhus

noviciate a novice in a religious order

civil to make frivolous objections

disgustingly aggravatingly

watering-place a fashionable holiday resort, where one could bathe in the sea, or bathe in or drink the waters of a mineral spring

300482

CHAPTER 21

- Emma makes amends to the Bates though she still is careless in the way she treats Harriet.

CONTEXT

The draper sold all the requirements for dressmaking; remember that in this period, there were no 'off the peg' clothes and young ladies either engaged a seamstress or made their own.

Following the evening with the Bates', Mr Knightley calls to congratulate Emma on her improved behaviour to Jane. He is disturbed to find that she still struggles with the same feelings, but her need for his approval is strong and she appeases any concerns he may have for her being uncharitable.

Emma has sent a large amount of pork to Miss Bates; as befits the daughter of the first family in the neighbourhood. Miss Bates and Jane visit to thank them and bring other news; Mr Elton is to be married to a Miss Hawkins of Bath. Emma is relieved at the news and amused at the speed with which he has got over his feelings for her.

Harriet has encountered Robert Martin and his sister in a local drapers shop and arrives at Hartfield in a flutter of spirits which concerns Emma greatly; so much so that she gives the news of Mr Elton's marriage in a blunter manner than planned.

GLOSSARY

spencer a woman's close-fitting jacket

'our lot is cast in a goodly heritage' misquotation from the Bible (Psalms 16:7), 'The lot is fallen unto me in a fair ground; yea, I have a goodly heritage'

COMMENTARY

In spite of mounting evidence of the unreliability of Emma's judgement, she persists in the fiction that Robert Martin is not good enough for Harriet, and her arrogance insists that the family hoped to gain by an alliance with a friend of Emma Woodhouse. However, she is concerned by the obvious gentility and sensitivity displayed in Robert Martin's encounter with Harriet; her worries mask a deep-seated suspicion that she may be wrong about the Martins.

CHAPTER 22

- Mr Elton returns, and Harriet is reminded of Robert Martin.

Mr Elton arrives home, full of self-importance and pride; a very different man to the one who left a few weeks before. Emma struggles to remember why she ever thought he was a gentleman in the first place, notwithstanding the obvious distasteful memories that his presence produces for her.

His bride is praised highly around the neighbourhood although she has not yet arrived. Her social status arises from connection with a brother-in-law of high standing in the community of Bath; she apparently has little else to recommend her.

Harriet receives a visit from Robert Martin's sisters; although she is out, they leave a calling card and Emma resolves that the visit must be duly returned. She is determined that the visit provide a balance of courtesy and distance; she has no desire for the former intimacy between Harriet and the Martins to be encouraged.

COMMENTARY

Formal social visiting was an important part of society, and there were rules accorded to carrying out the function. It would be seen as an unpardonable slight to ignore a visit paid, which explains Emma's consternation.

GLOSSARY

a Bristol-merchant, of course, he must be called the narrator hesitates before describing Miss Hawkins's father as a merchant, because it was considered very ungentlemanly to be 'in trade'

CHAPTER 23

- Harriet pays a visit to the Martins.
- There is welcome news from Frank Churchill.

Emma delivers Harriet to the Martins to return their visit. Her carriage is waiting after a prompt fifteen minutes; the time judged necessary to pay due courtesy without appearing familiar. Harriet feels it passed tolerably well, but Emma is concerned by an apparent reappearance of the old warmth at the very moment when she arrives to release her friend from their company.

Emma is in a very depressed state, battling with the dual preoccupations of the Martins and Mr Elton, and is very glad to bump into Mr and Mrs Weston to hear the joyous news that Frank Churchill is to arrive tomorrow for a fortnight's visit. She is excited to meet him and very glad at last that he will grace Mrs Weston with his presence.

Chapter 23 continued

Frank arrives earlier than expected, and shortly after his arrival is brought by his father to Hartfield. Emma is impressed by his courtesy and desire to make a good impression. He praises everything he sees without sycophancy and she has no doubt as to his sincerity but is slightly reserving judgement.

He mentions the need to pay a courtesy visit to his acquaintance Jane Fairfax, and when seeming to demur as to the necessity, his father is prompted to encourage him to pay his respects immediately.

COMMENTARY

Having had warning of Emma's tendency to misjudgement, readers are more on their guard in Volume II. Her interpretation of the behaviour and feelings of others has proved errant, therefore her views of the conduct and thoughts of Frank Churchill are more scrupulously attended to.

CHAPTER 24

- Emma becomes more disposed to approve of Frank Churchill.

The very next day brings Frank Churchill again, this time with Mrs Weston. Emma accompanies them into town for a tour of Highbury and is very impressed by Frank's approval of everything that he sees. He is particularly impressed with the dimensions of the local inn, and wonders why Emma has never encouraged the holding of balls there. He is clearly a social, fun-loving gentleman, very much like his father.

He remarks on the length of the visit he was required to pay to the Bates the day before; in spite of Emma's warning him of the need to be on his guard against the loquacious tongue of Miss Bates, he was trapped there for three quarters of an hour. Emma can readily believe him, having suffered from the same dilemma herself. Of course his real reason for staying so long is not guessed at, and he is fortunate to have so ready an excuse.

CONTEXT

Formal parties, or balls, were a regular social occurrence in the eighteenth and nineteenth centuries. They consisted of formal dancing, card games – usually bridge – and a late supper. The dancing was an opportunity for young ladies to display their grace and elegance.

Emma engages him in further questioning about Miss Fairfax and the Campbells, convinced as she is that there is an attachment between the son in law and Jane. Frank disputes this but readily engages in disapproval of Jane's reserve: Emma's principal criticism. He asks for Emma's opinion of Jane's abilities on the piano and Emma reassures him that Jane is a highly accomplished pianist.

COMMENTARY

Both Emma and Frank appear to share a keen interest in Jane Fairfax, which suits Emma's fascination with Jane and desire to discover something less than perfect about her. Her motivation is pure envy, whereas Frank's interest is far kinder.

CHAPTER 25

- Frank goes to London for a haircut.

Emma is rather disconcerted to hear that Frank Churchill has taken off the next day for London to have his hair cut. She feels it rather frivolous of him and rather less than she had expected. Mrs Weston feels the same, although his father laughs the tale off as a mark of the impetuosity of youth. Mr Knightley, not predisposed towards Frank in the first place, condemns the action as the mark of an insensitive, thoughtless youngster.

Emma is annoyed at the presumption of a local couple, the Coles, who have recently gained considerable trade wealth and have organised a party to which the Westons and Mr Knightley are invited. She is determined to refuse her own invitation should it arrive, yet is perversely offended when it doesn't. She has no intention of accepting and feels that the Coles are attempting to rise above their station by offering such an offensive invitation; something which her friends are clearly insensible to.

When the expected card does appear, she is quickly persuaded to accept, not wanting to be left out. Mr Woodhouse declines his own invitation on the grounds that he is an 'invalid' (p. 158), and

GLOSSARY

post-horses horses ready to be ridden forward to the next 'stage' with mail, and to furnish a change of horses for the coach carrying the mail

his indifference to a confusion of rank, bordered too much on inelegance of mind Emma thinks that Frank Churchill almost lacks refinement because he is willing to mix well-born people with their inferiors

cried up praised

repulsive unattractive

CONTEXT

Money derived from trade was a relatively new phenomenon, caused by the growth of the Industrial Revolution. To the landed gentry, whose wealth was derived from centuries of land ownership, it was perceived as a vulgar means of acquiring wealth.

attempts to discourage the others for attending also in the light of his own dislike of parties. However, his feelings are eventually assuaged and Emma, as usual, gets her own way.

COMMENTARY

Emma appears to have very delicate sensibilities regarding position in society; a very marked sensitivity in comparison with The Knightleys and the Westons. This peculiarly refined snobbery lies at the root of many of the scrapes she blunders into; particularly regarding her interference between Harriet and the Martins.

CHAPTER 26

- Emma graciously accepts an invitation to dinner.

Frank Churchill returns from London with the haircut, which was his apparent reason for so sudden a disappearance. It is the day of the dinner engagement at the Coles', and Emma is very much looking forward to spending an evening being admired and entertained.

She is not disappointed. Mr and Mrs Cole make it clear that she has honoured them by graciously accepting their invitation and defer enough to make Emma feel the guest of honour at the party.

She is pleased to see Frank again, and the two sit together at dinner; Emma musing aloud as to the mystery sender of a brand new piano which has arrived, anonymously, for Jane Fairfax. Emma is convinced that the present is a gift of love from Mr Dixon. Frank concurs with her idea immediately: 'Now I can see it in no other light but as an offering of love' (p. 165). The immense **irony** of this passage is developed throughout the chapter, as Emma plunges further and further into misconception. The reader is given several hints as to the real giver of the piano, and the real focus for Frank's affection; however Emma is as yet blinded by her own beliefs of astuteness into oblivious disregard for what is under her nose.

Mrs Weston confides to Emma her suspicions that Mr Knightey is falling in love with Jane Fairfax. Emma is extremely disapproving of this idea, finding the idea of 'a Mrs Knightey for them all to give way to!' (p. 172) completely intolerable. She puts her disapprobation down to fears for her nephew Henry's inheritance. Determined to prove her friend wrong, she pays particular attention to the way in which Mr Knightley observes Jane at the piano after dinner. She is quickly convinced that he has no romantic feelings for her at all, and her mind is at rest.

COMMENTARY

Young ladies were encouraged to learn to sing and play the piano. Evening entertainments of this kind were common practice amongst those circles inhabited by Emma's society. It was an expectation that young ladies learned the piano as well as embroidery, drawing, and painting. Emma is not insensible to her lack of skill on the piano compared to Jane; the major example of differing levels of accomplishment between them.

This chapter is heavy with **dramatic irony**. The reader, as observer of the action, can view from the perspective intended by Austen to give the most clarity. Frank's words, tone, facial expression and even position in the room is given in enough detail for us to gain a clear sense of the reality of his affections. As a central chapter, it is interesting that this one is so heavily peppered with ironic moments.

> **GLOSSARY**
>
> **spinet** a small musical instrument similar to a harpsichord

CHAPTER 27

- Miss Bates dominates the conversation.

The day after the party, Emma remembers with pleasure the pleasant evening she had; her pleasure largely derived from being the centre of attention. Complete pleasure is marred by the knowledge of the inferiority of her piano playing compared with Jane Fairfax. She diligently practices for an hour and a half to attempt to redress the lack of application of her youth. She also retains a shred of uneasiness from stating her suspicions regarding Jane and Mr Dixon to Frank Churchill, and resolves to say no more on that subject, whatever private suspicions she may cherish.

She goes with Harriet into Highbury and bumps into Frank Churchill and Mrs Weston, on their way to pay an apparently promised visit to the Bates' and Jane to hear the new piano. Emma and Harriet are persuaded into accompanying them.

COMMENTARY

Once again, Frank can be seen having manipulated his way into another opportunity to spend time with Jane Fairfax; Mrs Weston had made no such promise of a morning visit to Miss Bates.

We hear another delightful example of Miss Bates' ability to steer a course through a myriad of subjects with hardly a pause for breath. The chapter is dominated by an incessant **stream of consciousness** as the poor woman tumbles verbally through her thoughts. The reader is treated to a lovely moment of **irony** in Emma's comment regarding Miss Bates attempting to go back to a subject earlier mentioned; 'Emma wondered on what, of all the medley, she would fix'.

> **GLOSSARY**
>
> **figured** patterned
> **closet** cupboard

CHAPTER 28

- Everyone is invited to admire the new piano.

Jane is clearly agitated and Emma conjectures that this must be a result of knowledge of the anonymous sender of the piano. Frank is courtesy itself to Emma, paying her a great deal of attention during the visit.

Frank, Emma and Jane's comments on the sender of the piano mask coded meaning. **Ironically** Emma, feeling herself to be fully informed and having correct suspicions, could not be further from the truth. Stolen glances and secret smiles between Frank and Jane she attributes to knowledge of the attachment between Jane and Mr Dixon; particularly when Frank's comment; 'True affection only could have prompted it' (p. 183), is greeted with a warm blush and smile from Jane.

Mr Knightley passes outside and Miss Bates, calling from the window, invites him in to join them and Emma; which he appears about to do until she mentions that Frank Churchill is also there.

He hurries away directly, as do the guests when Miss Bates appears about to repeat the whole of the conversation again to them.

COMMENTARY

Mr Knightey's abruptness is mediated by his solicitude to the Bates; his gift of a large store of apples from his own orchards. He is clearly less than impressed with Frank Churchill; his attentions to Emma appear to pique him particularly. He had every intention of accepting Miss Bates' invitation until he heard that Frank Churchill was also inside.

Austen's skill in highlighting personality through direct speech is heavily emphasised in this chapter; only Mr Knightley is possessed of the ability to deflect the chatter of Miss Bates without seeming rude.

GLOSSARY
deedily busily

CHAPTER 29

- Frank wants a party.

Having enjoyed one evening of entertainment, Frank is determined that it should be followed in similar form. He decides that they should hold a ball.

Mr Woodhouse needs a great deal of persuading that any form of entertainment such as this is a good idea; he is so concerned about draughts and fatigues that it takes everything in Emma's power to persuade him to agree.

Although Frank is determined, even he has to eventually accede to the bare facts that his father's house is simply too small. Not to be deterred however, he soon lights on another possibility; the room at The Crown which all feel would be a much better venue. He goes with Emma and the Westons to ascertain the suitability of the accommodation afforded there. Although Mrs Weston worries that there will not be enough space for a supper room and a card room, everyone else appears in complete accord that the space is perfect. However, Frank insists on fetching Miss Bates (and Jane Fairfax) to ask their views.

COMMENTARY

Emma is inclined to share in Frank's enthusiasm, not in small measure influenced by knowing she is a good dancer and will not be outshone by Jane Fairfax in this talent, unlike in her piano playing. Furthermore, she revels in the idea of her and Frank being seen as a couple at the dance; she has already formed an idea of the appropriacy of a match between them.

Frank secures Emma's hand for the opening dance at the ball, to the delight of Mr and Mrs Weston.

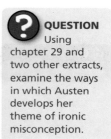

QUESTION
Using chapter 29 and two other extracts, examine the ways in which Austen develops her theme of ironic misconception.

Significance is attached to his request and her acceptance; believing it an indicator of an attachment between them. It was perceived as a great honour to be the couple starting off the dancing; this tradition remains in contemporary wedding receptions where the bride and groom lead off the dancers at the start of the evening.

CHAPTER 30

- Frank is summoned back to Enscome, and the party is postponed.

As soon as all the arrangements are in place, Emma becomes concerned at Mr Knightley's negative attitude to the ball. He sees no reason for it at all, and impresses upon her what a waste of an evening it will be for him. Emma is hurt by his apparent attack on her love for dancing, although relieved that it is a further sign that he clearly has no strong feelings for Jane Fairfax.

However, Frank is summoned back to Enscome; his aunt is unwell and he has to leave immediately. Emma is devastated – all hopes of the ball are now crushed.

He pays a speedy visit to Hartfield to say goodbye. During the conversation, he appears to be on the verge of imparting some confidence to Emma which she deftly steers him from, assuming it would be a declaration of his feelings for her. Once alone, she muses on her depressed state and resolves that she must be in love with Frank.

COMMENTARY

Emma expects that Mr Knightley will be pleased to hear that the ball is no longer taking place, but instead he is warmly sympathetic to her feelings and concerned for her disappointment. In spite of his distrust and disapproval of Frank Churchill, he displays the capacity to put Emma's feelings first.

This chapter has its **dramatic irony**. The reader suspects that Frank Churchill's attraction to Highbury may have rather more to do with Jane Fairfax than Emma, but Emma is blissfully unaware.

? QUESTION
Examine how Austen uses dramatic irony to involve the reader in the understanding of character in 'Emma'.

CHAPTER 31

* Emma hatches another plan.

Emma examines her feelings closely. She assumes she must be in love with Frank Churchill; he is an attractive man, their temperaments are well-suited, it is a match expected and wished for by the Westons. However, she is surprised to find that her life continues as contentedly in his absence as it did in his presence. Furthermore, the fantasies she indulges in whereby he makes declarations of love to her, are always refused. When she notices this, confusion over her feelings for the gentleman evaporate and she concludes that she feels nothing more than the warmth and regard for a friend.

Harriet continues her mourning for Mr Elton. The gentleman is expected to return to Highbury with his new bride any day, and Harriet beleaguers Emma with mention of the gentleman's name. Emma's patience, notwithstanding her resolution to suffer anything to aid Harriet get over Mr Elton, finally gives way and she points out to Harriet that continued mention of the subject pains herself, knowing as she does that she must take full responsibility for Harriet's attachment. Harriet, shocked and sorry, resolves never to mention his name again.

Emma cannot resist the idea that making another match for Harriet would be the best way to cure her of her feelings for Mr Elton, and, freed herself from emotional attachment to Frank Churchill, settles that he and her friend would make a charming couple.

COMMENTARY

Frank sends a courteous letter to Mrs Weston which Emma reads, scanning the pages for complimentary mentions of her own name. Frank pays due regard for protocol in this letter: the common means of communication in the nineteenth century.

The full warmth of Emma's affection appears best encountered when she is being praised. Harriet's protestations of undying regard and gratitude prompt the strongest feelings of love from Emma.

CHAPTER 32

- Mr Elton brings his bride home.

Mr Elton arrives, triumphant, with his bride. All of Highbury are full of curiosity to meet the lady. Emma decides to pay as speedy a visit as possible so as not to appear rude, and resolves that Harriet shall accompany her; therefore getting most of the initial embarrassment over with straight away. Mr Elton is gruff and embarrassed, but Emma is sensitive enough to recognise what a trial the visit must be for him.

The first visit is short, but when it is repaid Emma has greater leisure to judge her new neighbour. She finds her overfamiliar and crass. Although Emma has a particularly refined sense of her own importance, she is not mistaken in the dislike she takes to Mrs Elton who is portrayed as an insensitive, arrogant and haughty woman with little genuine taste or refinement.

Emma is particularly affronted by Mrs Elton's reference to 'Knightley' being 'quite the gentleman' (p. 210) as if she is surprised. Her outrage is clear and heartfelt, only stopped when she wonders what Mr Churchill would make of the insufferable woman. She immediately catches herself out thinking of him and ponders on how he is first in her mind, when in fact it is Mr Knightley occupying her thoughts and her strongest emotions all the time.

CONTEXT

The firstborn child of a gentleman would be referred to by their title and surname; younger siblings would be identified by their title, first name and surname. For example, Emma, as second-born child, is Miss Emma Woodhouse; her older sister Isabella was 'Miss Woodhouse' prior to her marriage.

COMMENTARY

This chapter illustrates the niceties of etiquette that distinguish gentry from the lower orders. Gentry referred to each other by their surname and title; it was considered overfamiliar in the extreme for first names to be used amongst acquaintances, and only gentlemen reserved the right to refer to each other by surname alone. Thus Mrs Elton breaks two societal codes almost immediately. Rigid social rules applied to the new bride: neighbours would first visit her in her new home, and this would be followed up by her making visits to those who had visited her. The new wife would precede everyone entering a room or going in to dinner – even those who would normally have precedence over her.

CHAPTER 33

- Mrs Elton takes a dislike to Emma.

Mrs Elton takes an immediate interest in Jane Fairfax, almost at the same time that her and her husband's behaviour towards Emma and Harriet considerably cools. Emma is relieved, whilst left in no doubt that the misunderstanding between herself, Harriet and Mr Elton has been fully communicated by the latter to his bride.

Jane refuses a second invitation from the Campbells to join them in Ireland, and Emma muses over this with Mrs Weston and Mr Knightley. He points out to her that Jane's stay in Highbury would have been made far more palatable if she had shown warmer interest in Jane herself. The point is not lost on Emma, who feels his disapproval keenly.

Although painful for Emma, reluctant as she is to hear what may be the accuracy of Mrs Weston's suspicions, she pushes Mr Knightley further to declare his feelings for Jane and he finally catches her meaning and announces very clearly to her and Mrs Weston that he has no warmer feelings for Jane than simple regard. Emma is extremely relieved to hear this, although Mrs Weston remains unconvinced.

GLOSSARY

barouche-landau a four-wheeled carriage which can be driven closed or open in which two couples can sit facing each other

I condition for nothing else that is all I insist on

my caro sposo (Italian) a vulgar and affected way of referring to her 'dear husband'

nice fastidious

COMMENTARY

Although Emma remains unaware of the reason for her dislike of the idea of a match between Mr Knightley and Jane Fairfax, the reader may begin to suspect deeper motivation.

Emma's judgement is shown to be not totally unreliable. Mr Knightley and Mrs Weston share her distaste for Mrs Elton. Also, the criticisms levelled against Emma for her treatment of Jane are greeted with pain. She knows them to be just and fair, and accepts them without argument.

CHAPTER 34

- Jane Fairfax goes to the post office.

As the rest of Highbury are busy proffering invitations to the Eltons, Emma does her duty and arranges a dinner party for eight. She invites Jane Fairfax to make the eighth, sensible as she is of Mr Knightley's criticisms of her past conduct.

Jane has walked in the rain to the post office for a letter. This causes great consternation, Mrs Elton particularly voluble in her condemnation of Jane's lack of care for her health. Emma, however, observes that Jane clearly wanted the walk to the post office and is in a very good mood; clearly the trip proved profitable for her.

COMMENTARY

What may be perceived as ridiculous fuss must be seen in context. As mentioned earlier in days of delicate health and limited medical knowledge, excessive care was taken to avoid chills and colds. Young ladies were perceived to have extremely delicate constitutions, to be protected from the adverse effects of the elements. Jane would be mindful to care for her health, and has risked taking cold in order to receive a letter which must have great importance for her. Clearly she is expecting a letter from Frank and, as Emma rightly surmises, has received one.

CHAPTER 35

- A letter from Frank contains news of his return.

Mrs Elton takes pains to get Jane to herself when the ladies withdraw after dinner. Emma overhears her blatantly pushing Jane to make a decision regarding a governess situation, and in spite of Jane repeating her desire to do nothing at present, pushes her own opinions very disagreeably to the point where Emma wonders how Jane can bear it.

Mr Weston arrives from town with a letter from Frank, bearing the very good news that the Churchills are moving south for the weather and Frank will be able to visit his friends whenever he likes. Emma feels uncomfortable at the news and wonders why, having settled in her own mind that she is not in love with him. The news does not appear to go down very well with either Mr Woodhouse or Mr Knightley but, unperturbed, Mr Weston continues on his theme to his next audience, Mrs Elton.

COMMENTARY

Chapter 35 marks the penultimate chapter of Volume II, and shows the author's skilful manipulation of the plot. Anticipation of Frank Churchill's return will ensure that readers will eagerly await the contents of Volume III.

CHAPTER 36

- A conversational battle ensues.

Mr Weston and Mrs Elton engage in a conversation reminiscent of a sparring match; each full of their own thoughts and desirous of being heard. Mr Weston gives Mrs Elton an account of Frank's history, not scrupling to condemn Mrs Churchill for her behaviour towards him over the years.

 CHECK THE NET

Use a comprehensive online encyclopedia such as http://en.wikipedia.org to search for 'British Empire' with a history of Britain's role in the slave trade until its eventual abolishment.

GLOSSARY

human flesh…the slave trade moves to abolish the slave trade (closely associated with Bristol) were initially made in 1807, though it was not finally banished until 1834 in the British Empire at large. Here, Jane Fairfax compares the position of governess to that of a slave.

Chapter 36 continued

Mrs Elton, ever on the lookout for a compliment, refers every point in Mr Weston's account back to herself wherever there is an opening; 'He will find an *addition* to the society of Highbury when he comes again; that is, if I may presume to call myself an addition' (pp. 232-3). Her final point begins with the **ironic** comment on Mrs Churchill; 'I have quite a horror of upstarts' (p. 234).

John Knightley is preparing to leave again. His eldest two boys are being left at Hartfield for a holiday, and their father is concerned that Emma will have less time for them due to her increased social life. She laughs this off although Mr Knightley seems particularly interested in what she has to say, and pleased when she disclaims the observations.

COMMENTARY

The second volume of the novel has established all the major characters. Jane Fairfax, Frank Churchill and Mrs Elton have all made their appearance and most of the plot developments are set in place for Volume III, which, form dictates, will contain the crisis and dénouement.

CHAPTER 37

- Frank returns and Emma is sure that she does not love him (nor he love her).

Emma realises that her concern at the return of Frank is due to worry about his disappointment. She is convinced he is desperately in love with her and does not want to hurt him.

Frank arrives for the day, and hurries to Hartfield to pay his respects to Emma. She watches him carefully, sensitive to any signs of love. She is confident – determined this time to make her feelings clear – that he has received full knowledge of her own feelings.

After the short visit has been paid, Emma is much more settled than she was before. She feels that Frank is much less in love with her than he was previously, although there is an 'agitation' (p. 237) and 'restlessness' (p. 238) which she cannot attribute a cause to. He

GLOSSARY

a retired place a secluded place

Hymen's saffron robe Hymen was the ancient Greek god of marriage and is referred to in John Milton's poem L'Allegro: 'let Hymen oft appear/In saffron robe.. Mrs Elton means 'before we married' leaves early, wanting to pay a courtesy call to a 'group of old acquaintance' (p. 238) before returning to London and his aunt.

Mrs Churchill does not settle in London and the family remove to Richmond, which is much nearer Highbury. Mr Weston is delighted, knowing that nothing can now stop Frank from visiting whenever he wishes. Plans for the ball at the Crown, abandoned in February, are now resumed and everyone is very excited.

COMMENTARY

There is much **dramatic irony** in this short chapter which opens Volume III. We the readers know the reason for Frank Churchill's unfulfilled promises and absences; Emma does not. The sense of anticipation continues, as preparations are renewed for the delayed ball.

CHAPTER 38

- Harriet is rescued by Mr Knightley.

The day of the ball arrives and Emma is invited by Mr Weston to arrive early and give her opinion on the décor and arrangements. She is slightly insulted to discover that he has extended the same invitation to several other families, and feels the slight of not being first in his regard.

Frank is delighted to see her, but once again appears restless. Mr and Mrs Elton, who were to bring Miss Bates and Jane, arrive without them and the carriage is sent back straight away. Frank appears eager to wait for them and escort them into the ballroom.

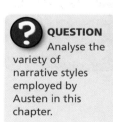

QUESTION
Analyse the variety of narrative styles employed by Austen in this chapter.

Emma is very interested to hear what Mr Churchill will make of Mrs Elton, and is soon gratified. The pair are inadvertently placed to overhear a conversation between the lady and 'Jane'; Frank appears to find the use of Jane's name in that manner highly offensive.

Mrs Weston, sensitive to decorum, realises that Mrs Elton (as bride) must be asked to start off the ball. Frank refuses to partner her, having made his engagement to Emma. In the end his father has the honour, and Mrs Elton is highly gratified at once again being first in company.

As the ball gathers pace, Emma notices that Harriet is not dancing. So does Mrs Weston, who entreats Mr Elton to partner her. When he deliberately snubs Harriet, much to Mrs Weston's shock and dismay, Emma is mortified. She notices gleeful smiles passing between Mr Elton and his wife. He sits himself beside Mr Knightley, who does not dance.

Emma cannot believe her eyes when she turns again and sees Mr Knightley escorting Harriet to the dance floor, and Mr Elton retreating to the card room in shame.

As soon as she gets the opportunity, Emma thanks him for his kindness to Harriet. He is disgusted with the behaviour of the Eltons and is quick to guess at the real reason for their unkindness to Harriet, and coolness towards Emma. She readily blames herself, but Mr Knightley feels that she has learned her own lesson and that her 'serious spirit' (p. 249) will lead her right. She asks him to ask her to dance, which he readily agrees to.

COMMENTARY

Emma clearly struggles with the social necessity of giving way to Mrs Elton at every function. Although the two women are very different, there is an obvious point of similarity in their shared need to be the centre of attention. Poor Emma does not find it easy to let someone else precede her, especially when the person is as distasteful as Mrs Elton.

Mr Knightley shows heightened sensitivity to the needs and feelings of those around him in his actions in this chapter. He acts graciously towards Harriet, rescuing her from extreme embarrassment by asking her to dance. He does this in spite of his own reluctance for dancing.

Notice Jane Austen's very clever way of mixing snatches of dialogue to create a sense of excited socialising and bustle – almost similar to the later 'stream of consciousness' style adopted by such writers as James Joyce and Virginia Woolf.

CHAPTER 39

- Harriet is rescued by Frank.

Emma remembers Mr Knightley's behaviour with great pleasure the following day. It is highly gratifying to her to know that he shares her opinion of the Eltons. His compliments to Harriet also give Emma pleasure; he clearly does not want to quarrel with her as in the past he was wont.

Although the Eltons have behaved appallingly towards Harriet, Emma feels sure that such rudeness will serve to cure Harriet of her infatuation with Mr Elton.

Suddenly, Frank Churchill and Harriet appear; Harriet fainting away as soon as she gets to a chair. She has been attacked by a band of gypsies, and Frank, who just happened to be on the same road, saved her and brought her to Hartfield. As soon as the fuss and shock are over, it occurs to Emma that this circumstance is highly likely to bring about feelings of romance between Frank and Harriet. However, she resolves not to interfere by word or deed.

COMMENTARY

Is Emma at last showing signs of maturity by not pushing the Harriet–Frank encounter, or is she so strongly convinced of her own conviction that something may come of it that she does not feel the need?

CHAPTER 40

- Harriet finally recovers.

Harriet visits, bearing a parcel of '*Most precious treasures*' (pp. 254–5) which she wants Emma to witness her burn. The parcel contains a piece of plaster that Mr Elton played with once, and a piece of old pencil which once belonged to him. Emma is torn between shame and amusement as she witnesses Harriet's attachment to these objects, and discovering therefore how strong her attachment to

> **CONTEXT**
>
> To a society governed by strict, immovable rules of status and behaviour, the notion of a gypsy represented complete anathema. Gypsies lived outside these codes; they were classless, did not own land, and moved from place to place.

> **GLOSSARY**
>
> **sweep-gate** drive gate

Mr Elton must have been. Harriet solemnly burns the relics of her lost love, and Emma feels sure that any attachment to Mr Elton is now over.

Although she has resolved to herself never to interfere again and keep to herself any wishes for Harriet and Frank Churchill, she cannot help herself when she and Harriet are discussing marriage a few days later.

Harriet resolves never to marry, stating that she will merely 'admire him at a distance' (p. 257). Emma assumes she means Frank, especially when she refers to the service he performed for Harriet and hearing her delighted concurrence. Emma is referring to the incident with the gypsies; it never crosses her mind that Harriet may be speaking of something (and someone) else.

Emma's advice to Harriet is to not despair of the hopelessness of the match; that 'matches of greater disparity have been made' (p. 258), and that she should monitor his behaviour towards her carefully for any sign of return of affection. Due to the blunders of the past, she resolves that no name should pass between them; therefore has no idea of whom Harriet means.

COMMENTARY

Emma's new-found sensibility to not interfering cannot be sustained. She is giving advice to Harriet in the midst of protestations of not interfering; in full knowledge that Harriet will be completely guided by what she thinks and feels.

Once again Jane Austen is having teasing fun with her characters.

CHAPTER 41

- Mr Knightley suspects double dealing.

Mr Knightley becomes suspicious of an attachment between Jane Fairfax and Frank Churchill. He observes looks of understanding pass between them during a dinner at the Eltons. Once his suspicions are aroused he is mindful of further hints.

> **GLOSSARY**
>
> **court plaister** silk sticking plaster
>
> **spruce-beer** beer made from the needles and small branches of spruce

During an evening at Hartfield, Frank betrays the fact that he is receiving news from Highbury from another source than herself. Although he glosses over his mistake quickly enough to fool the others, Mr Knightley misses none of the intelligence which passes between Frank and Jane.

His antipathy towards Frank can only be increased in his suspicions that he is dealing double with Emma's feelings. It appears clear to him, as to the Westons, that Frank intends to propose to Emma and Mr Knightley is deeply suspicious of his motives in his secret communication with Jane.

Mr Knightley, as a friend, attempts to warn Emma of the danger she is placing herself in but she does not listen. She gives no credence to Mr Knightley's suspicions as she believes herself fully in the confidence of Frank Churchill.

COMMENTARY

Of course it never occurs to Emma that there may be understandings between others that she is not privy to. Once again, Mr Knightley's judgement is proving trustworthy and accurate; he is far more astute that Emma, who prides herself on being the best judge of character. This is the first time we are privy to what Mr Knightley is thinking.

> **GLOSSARY**
>
> **'Myself creating what I saw'** quotation from the eighteenth-century poet William Cowper's The Task
>
> **Pembroke** small table with two flaps

CHAPTER 42

- Plans are made for a picnic.

Mrs Elton waits in vain for a visit from her sister and brother-in-law, the Sucklings. Lost for an opportunity to show off and preen her connections to money, she proposes that the plans to spend the day at Box Hill not be put off any longer.

Emma really wants to go to Box Hill, and she and Mr Weston decide to make their own arrangements for a picnic. However, Mr Weston, who can never resist the opportunity for a large party, suggests to Mrs Elton that the two groups join and go together. Although Emma cannot say so to Mr Weston, she is very unhappy about being seen to be a member of Mrs Elton's party, and is annoyed with his excessively sociable temper and undiscerning taste in people.

However, a lame horse causes the arrangements to be temporarily abandoned. Frustrated and annoyed, Mrs Elton turns to Mr Knightley in despair, who suggests that instead of exploring further afield, they all come to Donwell Abbey for a strawberry-picking picnic. Mrs Elton is delighted with this alternative plan and is on the verge of taking over all the arrangements for food and invitations in the height of arrogance, but Mr Knightley firmly puts her in her place.

Mrs Elton appears determined to continue to push Jane into making a decision about her future, and insists that she be allowed to help find her a governess position. Emma observes Jane's temper beginning to fray until she can stand no more and walks away.

Emma returns to the house to spend some time with her father and relieve Mrs Weston of the burden of keeping him company. She bumps into Jane who wants Emma to make her excuses; she is determined to leave alone and go home; evidently upset by something, which Emma feels sure is the unwanted attentions from Mrs Elton. She appeals to Emma to help her in making an unnoticed escape, which Emma is glad to do.

Frank arrives within moments of Jane's departure, clearly out of sorts and irritable. Emma tries to cheer him up by reminding him of the planned excursion to Box Hill the next day.

COMMENTARY

Mr Knightley's plans for the day show sensitivity to the needs and feelings of everyone, especially Mr Woodhouse. Emma finds great enjoyment in exploring Donwell Abbey again and spends her time admiring the pleasant house and extensive grounds.

During a walk in the grounds, Emma notices Mr Knightley and Harriet walking together and is pleasantly surprised and pleased. It is important to her that he likes Harriet, and she is glad to see that he is paying her attention – thoughts which future chapters will show to have a heavy **irony**.

GLOSSARY

Box Hill a popular beauty spot near Dorking in Surrey, which was a great favourite for picnic parties.

52 Emma

CHAPTER 43

- The expedition to Box Hill does not go smoothly.

The excursion to Box Hill does not live out its expectations of a pleasant diversion. Emma cannot understand why, but there appears to be a pall over the spirits of the party. Frank Churchill begins the day in a sombre, quiet mood; so much so that she is bored with his company and relieved when the group converge for lunch. Once seated, he becomes vibrant and flirtatious. In spite of receiving plenty of flattery, she is concerned that others will receive the impression that there is a romantic understanding between them.

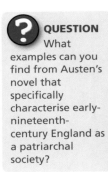

QUESTION
What examples can you find from Austen's novel that specifically characterise early-nineteenth-century England as a patriarchal society?

Because Emma is feeling depressed, she goes out of her way to appear more cheerful and gay than she actually feels. She makes a silly quip to Miss Bates about the extent of her prattling; once out of her mouth it cannot be recanted and Mr Knightley draws her aside to remonstrate.

He appears very concerned with Emma's behaviour and speaks warmly to her about the heartlessness of her comment. Emma is devastated by his words; she knows she has done an unpardonable wrong by insulting Miss Bates, but it is Mr Knightley's censure which upsets her far more greatly. The day ends miserably with Emma in floods of tears.

COMMENTARY

The reader has received enough hints now to be as aware as Mr Knightley that there is some kind of relationship between Jane Fairfax and Frank Churchill. Austen has made us aware in Volume I that Emma is far from being the astute judge of character and situation that she believes herself to be; she sees what she wants to see and what she believes is there. Mr Knightley, on the other hand, is very astute and his judgement has been proven correct on several counts already.

The Box Hill party is the pivotal example of Emma living at the centre of a web of **ironic** intrigue which she feels fully involved in but is completely mistaken about. To the reader, who knows enough about Mr Knightley's judgement to trust his suspicions regarding Jane and Frank, the behaviour of Frank and Jane clearly demonstrates that not only is there a relationship between them, but there has been some sort of argument. Frank's zealous attentions to Emma only begin when Jane is nearby and are clearly designed to make her jealous. Jane's comment about hasty engagements – one of the few times we have noticed her volunteer a remark in conversation – is one which he appears to understand the full meaning of.

CHAPTER 44

- Emma tries to make amends.

Chastened and subdued, Emma painfully mulls over the dreadful morning at Box Hill. Mr Knightley's disapproval of her conduct has hurt her deeply, and she fully acknowledges the correctness of his criticism. She resolves to pay a visit to Miss Bates directly, and in future to be far more attentive to the Bates.

Although somewhat reserved initially, Miss Bates soon forgets the slight and is grateful for Emma's visit. However Jane will not see her. Emma hears with dismay that she has very suddenly decided to accept the offer of a position as governess, engineered by Mrs Elton.

Emma's feelings for Jane have warmed considerably recently and she is very sympathetic to the young woman's plight. Her conversation with Miss Bates is full of genuine feeling and interest for Jane.

COMMENTARY

There is far more of the disingenuous in Emma than previously. She appears to have matured in the space of a few months from a self-absorbed, selfish and conceited young girl into a woman who cares more for the comfort and feelings of others than of herself. In her attentions to Miss Bates and changed feelings for Jane, she is finally exhibiting what Mr Knightley wished for her.

GLOSSARY

John Ostler John the stable man at the inn

CHAPTER 45

- News of the death of Mrs Churchill arrives.

Mr Knightley is waiting for her when she returns home. He plans to visit his brother in London and wanted to see her to say goodbye before he left. When he hears from Mr Woodhouse that Emma has been to call on Miss Bates, he understands completely the reasoning behind the visit and looks at her with warm approbation.

News arrives from Richmond that Mrs Churchill has died suddenly; Frank's most recent peremptory summons home appears this time to have had good cause. Although the normal respects to the departed are paid, Emma cannot help rejoicing in the fact that Frank is now free from his encumbrance to his aunt and at liberty to marry Harriet.

Jane Fairfax continues to be unwell. Mr Perry is sent for, and reports to Emma and her father that Jane's spirits seem to be so depressed that she may be unable to take up her new position as soon as she would have wished.

COMMENTARY

Emma is determined to redress past slights to Jane. She makes repeated attempts to call on her but all of them are avoided under the premise of Jane's being unequal to company. When Emma finds out that Jane has being admitting other friends, she is hurt but not surprised. She knows her motives are genuine and is aware that it may be too late for her to form a friendship with Jane.

Much of Emma's actions stem from a genuine desire to offer friendship to Jane; however there is the other motive of wanting Mr Knightley's approbation of her behaviour. The knowledge that she is acting and feeling honourably does much to comfort her in spite of the curtness with which Jane rejects her attempts.

> **CONTEXT**
>
> Austen's focus on the dynamics of friendships, relationships and family is a key characteristic of her work.

CHAPTER 46

- The secret engagement is revealed.

CONTEXT

Formal permission for marriage had to be obtained from the legal guardian of any person under the age of twenty-one.

Ten days after the death of Mrs Churchill, Mr Weston arrives at Hartfield. He is clearly very upset, and entreats Emma to return with him immediately to Randalls. Emma is panicked by his refusal to tell her what is the matter straight away, insisting that she hear it from his wife. He reassures her that the news has nothing to do with her family, but will say no more until they arrive at his home.

Mrs Weston is just as upset as her husband. She tells Emma that Frank Churchill and Jane Fairfax have been secretly engaged for months – well before both arrived at Highbury. The death of Frank's aunt has freed him from her censure, and his uncle has been kinder in giving instant permission for the engagement to be made public.

The primary concern of the Westons is Emma's feelings; believing as they did that Frank's attentions to her were more meaningful than they actually were. Emma is quick to reassure them that they have nothing to concern themselves about on her account, and that she has only feelings of friendship for Frank; nothing more.

She is, however, quick to condemn Frank's behaviour and is also immediately sensitive to Jane's feelings in Frank's attentions to herself. She is also concerned that she has let her own tongue run away with her with regard to the suspicions she has communicated to Frank about Jane and Mr Dixon. And above all, she is once again concerned for Harriet, whose disappointment will be most acute.

COMMENTARY

It is interesting to note the change in Emma in her reaction to this news. Her primary thoughts are for the feelings of Harriet and Jane: for Harriet's disappointment and for Jane being put in the position of daily witnessing Frank flirting openly with herself. She is quickest to condemn Frank on this point; she sympathises with Jane completely now she understands what Frank was doing and does not approve.

A secret engagement was not something approved of in this society. Although romantic, it placed the lady particularly in an uncomfortable position and was felt to be deceptive and to be regarded with suspicion. The usual reason for such an arrangement was because the marriage would be disapproved of, either by society in general or by the family of one or both parties. As it was considered extremely disrespectful to go against the wishes of one's eldest and betters, it was highly unlikely that a secret engagement could ever be viewed in less than condemnatory terms.

CHAPTER 47

- Emma receives the shocking truth of Harriet's affection.

Emma's concern for the feelings of Jane Fairfax is quickly dissipated by worry for Harriet. With genuine, honest assessment of her behaviour, she acknowledges her part in once again encouraging Harriet to fall in love.

She is astonished when Harriet arrives at Hartfield, full of the news about Frank and Jane but exhibiting none of the despair which Emma was sure she would be feeling. When Emma expresses her surprise, it is not long before she establishes, with great shock, that Harriet is not in love with Frank at all; she is in love with Mr Knightley. He is the unnamed gentleman they have spoken of. The great service rendered Harriet, which partly caused this swell of love, was not Frank rescuing her from the gypsies, but Mr Knightley asking her to dance after Mr Elton snubbed her at the ball.

With an acuity of feeling unusual for Emma, the shock of this news causes her to look instantly into her own heart and recognise that she is in love with Mr Knightley herself; in fact, she has been for a long time. She realises that he has always been the yardstick by which she has measured every other gentleman she meets, and his opinion of her is the most important one in the world; more important even than her father or Mrs Weston as it is honest and clear as well as loving. She cannot tolerate the idea of Mr Knightley being sunk to such an extent by an alliance with Harriet.

Chapter 47 continued

However, she acknowledges that none of this is Harriet's fault, and that she has to behave like a good friend. Therefore, in spite of her inner turmoil, she collects herself enough to draw Harriet to tell her everything about Mr Knightley's behaviour towards her and why she feels her feelings are returned. In spite of herself, she has to acknowledge that there is some substance in Harriet's words.

COMMENTARY

This chapter displays the extent to which Emma has matured and grown. Primarily this is through her inner revelation of feelings for Mr Knightley, but also through her assessment of her behaviour towards Harriet. She fully acknowledges that she has been the instigator in creating vanity and pride in Harriet; that she has encouraged her to think of herself as better than she is. Emma sincerely mourns the fact that she did not leave Harriet alone, and that had she done so, Harriet would have now been happily married to Robert Martin.

She fully acknowledges her own mistakes; 'With insufferable vanity had she believed herself in the secret of everybody's feelings; with unpardonable arrogance proposed to arrange everybody's destiny' (p. 312). Because she is first to admit her errors, the reader is allowed to sympathise with rather than condemn her behaviour.

> **QUESTION**
> Which character undergoes the most drastic transformation in the novel?

CHAPTER 48

- Emma feels hopeless, as she imagines life without Mr Knightley.

Emma spends the following day lost in troubled thought. Now the realisation has dawned upon her, she is finally fully sensible of how important Mr Knightley has always been to her. Although she hopes that Harriet may be mistaken in believing he loves *her*, she is under no illusion that he has any strong feelings for herself. She can only hope that he remains unmarried and that his relationship to their family continues as it has done from her childhood. She knows that she can never abandon her father by marrying, and merely wishes that the friendly relationship between them not be altered. Although previously she has renounced marriage as a means to happiness, claiming that she would never be as paramount in importance in any other situation as her current one, the reality is that she could never tolerate the idea of abandoning her father. Thus her real motivation is far more noble that she has previously admitted.

Mrs Weston, who has been to call on her prospective daughter-in-law, comes to see Emma. Emma listens, and attempts to be cheerful and interested; but this subject, once so interesting for her, cannot claim her attention now and her thoughts keep drifting back to Mr Knightley. When her friend leaves she is once more lost in thought of how badly she has behaved, and how well she might have done in taking Mr Knightley's advice in terms of her treatment of Jane.

Her day ends badly as she recognises how lonely and isolated her future will be at Hartfield, away from all the society she now holds so dear, in the full knowledge that this misery is 'all her own work' (p.320).

COMMENTARY

Although much matured, Emma is still unable to judge character as well as she believes. For instance, she does not consider that for Mr Knightley to remonstrate with her following her rudeness to Miss Bates, he must care considerably about the manner in which she conducts herself.

It is a very different Emma who responds with compassion and sensitivity to hearing of Jane's suffering over the preceding months of secret engagement, and who fully acknowledges her own part in creating the misery Jane must have undergone.

The dull and stormy summer weather serves as a **pathetic fallacy**, enhancing the gloomy mood of the central character. Emma's inner resources are fully tested as she attempts to comfort and entertain her grumpy father in spite of the misery she feels herself. This itself is a testament to the kinder side of her nature which still puts his feelings before her own.

> **CONTEXT**
>
> In the early-nineteenth-century a woman from the upper classes would not pursue a career and so sought marriage to a wealthy suitor as a way of securing her future.

CHAPTER 49

- A proposal is received and accepted.

The stormy July weather continues into the next day but begins to brighten towards evening. Emma, determined to seek relief from the oppression she has been suffering, walks in the garden. She is surprised to see Mr Knightley approach her, believing him to still be in London with her sister.

? QUESTION
To what extent do you think the culture of repression in early-nineteenth-century England controls the actions of the characters in the novel?

At first very formal and distant with each other, Emma is careful not to betray an ounce of her suspicions or her misery. She broaches the subject of the impending marriage between Frank and Jane, and Mr Knightley immediately takes the opportunity of warmly comforting her broken heart. He declares Frank to be a villain, insensitive and callous in the extreme. Completely confused for a moment, Emma realises that he assumed she loved Frank and is quick to dispel any misunderstanding whilst laying the blame fully at her own door for being flattered by his intentions and seeming to encourage them.

Mr Knightley, convinced at last that Emma is being truthful in her assertions, appears to want to open the subject of his own attachment but Emma cannot bear to hear him confide his love for Harriet and stops him from speaking further. When she sees how deeply hurt he is by her response, her need to remain his good friend conquers her own feelings and she presses him to continue.

When he does speak, Emma cannot believe her ears. His words are a proposal to her, not a confessing of feeling for her friend. Almost overcome by emotion, she hears with delight his protestations that he has always loved her, and waits only for her permission to continue.

Mr Knightley is similarly overcome, having suspected nothing of her feelings for him – indeed, assuming that she loved Frank. He admits that his motivation in leaving Highbury was to distance himself from daily observations of the growing attachment between Emma and Frank, and the only reason for return was to comfort Emma when the news of the engagement reached London.

COMMENTARY

Mr Knightley's unwillingness to see good in Frank Churchill is now understood as barely disguised jealousy. Just as Emma realised how she felt about Mr Knightley when someone else threatened their relationship, he first realised his love for her when Frank Churchill arrived in Highbury. It is testament to his genuine regard for her that his primary concern was for her happiness, at the expense, seemingly, of his own.

However Emma at this stage is to be equally praised for unselfishness; her desire to remain his friend and confidant put her in a potentially torturous situation, little suspecting that the revelations of his heart should pertain to her and not Harriet. There is a balance, an equity in their situation and sensitivity to each other which makes the match between them much more suited and satisfactory.

As testament to how genuinely Emma now thinks of others, her overwhelming happiness is mediated almost instantly by thoughts of Harriet's feelings.

QUESTION
How does Austen show the extent to which Emma has matured through the course of the novel?

CHAPTER 50

- Frank explains all in a letter to Mrs Weston.

This chapter is almost completely taken over by a very long letter from Frank, delivered to Emma with a covering note from Mrs Weston who desires that she reads the missive immediately.

Before the letter arrives from Randalls, Emma has been busy attending to the feelings of the two people she is most concerned about; her father and Harriet. For her father, she resolves, painful as it is, that she can never leave Hartfield while he remains alive and that any wedding plans must be laid aside until then. For Harriet, she knows that she cannot put off the inevitable of communicating to her poor friend the astounding revelations of yesterday. She writes to her as sensitively as she can, explaining what has happened and at the same time securing an invitation for her to stay in London with Isabella and John.

The letter from Frank is a full explanation of his conduct over the preceding months; detailed and honest. Emma reads it, not with any desire to be further persuaded of his basic decency, but because Mrs Weston so strongly desired Frank to be understood and forgiven for his actions.

The letter gives a strong impression of how much Frank and Jane are in love and how they only entered into the engagement as a result of Mrs Churchill being so unreserved and selfish. A match between her nephew and a portionless governess would never have been approved. As this is thoroughly known and understood by all who knew the lady, it does part-way explain Frank's conduct. He takes the full blame for persuading Jane to enter into the engagement, insisting that it is he, and not she, who should suffer the censure of their friends. In fact it was she who decided that she could not bear the deceit any more and decided to break it off, which is why she accepted the governess position arranged by Mrs Elton. Frank explains that he received news of her decision on the day of his aunt's death, and, after asking for his uncle's consent, hurried to Highbury to beg her forgiveness and explain that they were now free to marry.

COMMENTARY

Frank's letter gives a third-hand account of a similar growing-up process to Emma's. It is by his open and honest acceptance of his wrongs, and desire to put them right, that forgiveness is possible. He has behaved badly, particularly regarding his treatment of Emma; but asserts honestly that had he ever received any intimation that she had strong feelings for him, he would never behaved in the way he did.

However, his open flirtation must have been almost impossible for Jane to bear; particularly cruel on the day of the Box Hill party when it was designed to hurt her after their quarrel. Emma is fully sensible to how she must have appeared to Jane as a rival.

Also, his selfishness is made apparent in the way he approaches his uncle immediately after the death of Mrs Churchill to get his consent to the marriage.

GLOSSARY

the event of the 26th ult. the day of Mrs Churchill's death

CHAPTER 51

> • Mr Knightley attempts to be kinder to Frank.

When Mr Knightley arrives, Emma insists that he read Frank's letter immediately: which he does, to please her. He reads the whole whilst providing a running commentary on how each part affects him. He is still not disposed to be generous to Frank, and is openly critical of his selfishness and wilful disregard of the feelings of others. Even the gift of the piano was, in Mr Knightley's eyes, a selfish act of love which paid no regard to how it was to be explained nor the inconvenience it would cause.

He finishes the letter little more disposed to be generous in his estimate of Frank's behaviour and character, and merely hopes that the constant society of Jane will provide the positive role model of sense and steadiness his immaturity needs.

Eager to be done with discussion of Frank Churchill, Mr Knightley communicates his concern over what is to be done about Mr Woodhouse. He agrees with Emma that it would be impossible to abandon the old gentleman; an equally unfeasible solution is the idea that both go to live at Donwell Abbey. His idea, then, is that for the remainder of Mr Woodhouse's life, Mr Knightley give up Donwell Abbey and live at Hartfield. Emma is staggered by how much indeed he must love her to sacrifice the comfort of his family home to spend his days with her.

COMMENTARY

The chapter ends with Emma, in spite of near-perfect happiness, brooding over what is to be done with Harriet; how her pain can possibly be assuaged.

The novel is gradually moving towards a happy closure, as one by one, problems begin to be resolved. Only the fate of Harriet – 'a loser in every way' (p. 340) and the knowledge that she must tell her father of Mr Knightley's declaration now remain unresolved.

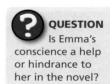

QUESTION
Is Emma's conscience a help or hindrance to her in the novel?

CHAPTER 52

- Emma visits Jane Fairfax.

Emma and Harriet have still not spoken, and Emma is relieved when Harriet takes up the offer of a visit to Isabella and John. Emma knows that she will have more distraction in London and more opportunities to have her spirits lifted.

She is dreading telling her father her news and would under normal circumstances prefer not to put it off. However, the impending birth of Mrs Weston's baby serves as a good excuse to say nothing until both mother and child are safe and well.

In the meantime, she resolves to visit Jane Fairfax and cement their friendship. She is very warmly greeted by the lady herself, but cannot have an open conversation with her because Mrs Elton is already ensconced on the sofa and determined to use every opportunity to drop enormous hints about her own knowledge of the mystery.

Emma bears all of this with good-humoured patience, even when Mrs Elton disagrees with her about the date of a meeting between her husband and Mr Knightley at the Crown. When Mr Elton himself arrives, she is shown to be wrong (again) but Emma says nothing.

Knowing that she cannot possibly have a proper conversation with Jane while the silly woman is there, Emma gets up to leave. She is escorted downstairs by Jane who evidently wishes to talk to her in private – or at least away from Mrs Elton. Outside, the two women finally make their peace in a warm mutual apology of past misconduct towards each other.

COMMENTARY

Mrs Elton's ridiculous behaviour serves only to make her look even more ludicrous than ever. Everyone in the room is aware of the 'secret' engagement; Jane and Miss Bates appear desperate to discuss and rejoice in the knowledge with Emma. Silly Mrs Elton, who has to puff herself up with importance whenever she has the opportunity, goes through a bizarre series of whispered hints and knowing looks which inhibits the others from having a proper conversation. Emma, who may in the past have been not unfairly compared with Mrs Elton in some respects, is now shown to be completely superior in conduct, manners and sense.

CHAPTER 53

- Emma tells her father of her engagement.

Emma is still worried about Harriet, and fears that Mr Knightley must suspect a cooling of friendship between them. John and Isabella are informed of the engagement and write their warmest approbation of the plan. They intend to visit Hartfield in August, bringing Harriet back with them.

Once Mrs Weston has safely had her baby, Emma and Mr Knightley judge that it is time for formal permission to be requested of Mr Woodhouse. Emma has dreaded this moment, knowing how it will upset her father and shake his nerves.

She is indebted to the assistance of her prospective husband and Mrs Weston, who both understand her father very well and skilfully manoeuvre him into a state of resigned acceptance of the plan.

Once Mr Weston receives the news, it very quickly spreads throughout Highbury as Emma and Mr Knightley knew it would – Mr Weston finding it impossible to keep a secret. The news is greeted warmly by everyone except Mrs Elton who pities 'poor Knightley' (p. 355) for his bad choice.

COMMENTARY

Of course it is inevitable that Mrs Elton should be annoyed; she already dislikes and envies Emma for her superior position in Highbury society, and marriage to the richest and most eligible bachelor in the area will only serve to raise that position further.

The author cannot resist the opportunity to flaunt the extent to which Mrs Elton suffers from self-delusion; 'How happy he had been to come and dine with them whenever they asked him!' (p. 355).

GLOSSARY

Madame de Genlis's *Adelaide and Theodore* published in 1783, this was a book by the French educationalist

CHAPTER 54

- Harriet is engaged.

Just before John, Isabella and Harriet are due to arrive at Hartfield, Mr Knightley tells Emma some news which he fears will distress her. Robert Martin has proposed again to Harriet and this time been accepted. Emma is delighted with this news, and can at last be completely happy now that concern for Harriet is no longer necessary. In complete good spirits, she goes with her fiance and Mr Woodhouse to visit Randalls. Frank and Jane arrive, and any initial awkwardness between her and Frank is soon removed.

Emma is overjoyed with the news about Harriet; she secretly suspected that Harriet had never lost her initial regard for Robert Martin in spite of Emma's efforts to persuade her otherwise. Her new-found maturity recognises the suitability of the match, and in an echoing of Mr Knightley's sentiments early in the novel, acknowledges that Harriet could not have made a more appropriate match for her situation in society. Mr Knightley is very surprised and relieved by Emma's reaction. Her honest explanation for the change is that she was a 'fool' (p. 367) previously.

> **GLOSSARY**
>
> **Astley's** a circus founded in 1798 and performed at the Royal Amphitheatre

During a friendly conversation with Frank which does much to disperse any awkwardness between them, her overriding impression of him is how infinitely inferior in sense and worth is he to her Mr Knightley.

CHAPTER 55

- The couples get married.

In the true style of a romantic novel, the last chapter is reserved for the nuptial celebrations; in this case, three-fold. Harriet and Emma meet and all former warmth between them is restored. Robert Martin proves to be everything Mr Knightley said he was; a man of taste and decency. Emma is aware that the nature of the friendship between her and Harriet cannot be maintained in the light of their differing status but is sincerely happy that her friend has found happiness in spite of her interference.

Harriet turns out to be the illegitimate daughter of a tradesman; very far from the nobleman's daughter Emma had persuaded herself she was. She is finally able to laugh at herself for being so misguided and selfishly motivated, and only glad that she was spared the pain of lasting damage caused by her persistent interference in the lives of others.

Harriet and Robert are married by Mr Elton. Emma and Mr Knightley plan to marry soon afterwards, taking advantage of the time while John and Isabella are still at Hartfield. They despair, however, of ever being able to persuade Mr Woodhouse to agree to a date – until Mrs Weston's chicken-house is conveniently robbed and Mr Woodhouse can only be made to feel safe with the knowledge of Mr Knightley's presence in the house to protect them all.

COMMENTARY

Mrs Elton, who always demands the last word, is given such in her condemnation of the wedding clothes; 'Very little white satin, very few lace veils; a most pitiful business!' (p. 367). However the narrator, with the omniscience of time as well as place, assures the reader that in spite of lack of outward show, the marriage proceeded in 'perfect happiness' (p. 367). It is noticeable that none of the central characters are given voice in this chapter; once their happiness is settled they need have nothing further to say. Furthermore, this technique distances them slightly from the reader, which is appropriate as their story is about to end.

EXTENDED COMMENTARIES

TEXT 1 – CHAPTER 1 (PP. 5–6)

Emma Woodhouse, handsome, clever, and rich, with a comfortable home and happy disposition, seemed to unite some of the best blessings of existence; and had lived nearly twenty-one years in the world with very little to distress or vex her.

She was the youngest of the two daughters of a most affectionate, indulgent father, and had, in consequence of her sister's marriage, been mistress of his house from a very early period. Her mother had died to long ago for her to have more than an indistinct remembrance of her caresses, and her place had been supplied by an excellent woman as governess, who had fallen little short of a mother in affection.

Sixteen years had Miss Taylor been in Mr Woodhouse's family, less as a governess than a friend, very fond of both daughters, but particularly of Emma. Between *them* it was more the intimacy of sisters. Even before Miss Taylor had ceased to hold the nominal office of governess, the mildness of her temper had hardly allowed her to impose any restraint; and the shadow of authority now log passed away, they have been living together as friend and friend very mutually attached, and Emma doing just what she liked; highly esteeming Miss Taylor's judgement, but directed chiefly by her own.

The real evils indeed of Emma's situation were the power of having rather too much her own way, and a disposition to think a little too well of herself; these were the disadvantages which threatened alloy to her many enjoyments. The danger, however, was at present so unperceived, that they did not by any means rank as misfortunes with her.

Sorrow came – a gentle sorrow – but not at all in the shape of any disagreeable consciousness – Miss Taylor married. It was Miss Taylor's loss which first brought grief. It was on the wedding-day of this beloved friend that Emma first sat in mournful thought of any continuance. The wedding over and the bride-people gone, her father and herself were left to dine together, with no prospect of a third to cheer a long evening. Her father composed himself to sleep after dinner, as usual, and she had then only to sit and think of what she had lost.

The event had every promise of happiness for her friend. Mr Weston was a man of unexceptionable character, easy fortune, suitable age and pleasant manners; and there was some satisfaction in considering with what self-denying, generous

CONTEXT

The novel's plot concerns Emma's education as she evolves from the spoilt young girl described in the opening chapters and gradually learns of the pitfalls that her pursuit of self-satisfaction brings.

friendship she had always wished and promoted the match; but it was a black morning's work for her. The want of Miss Taylor would be felt every hour of every day. She recalled her past kindness – the kindness, the affection of sixteen years – how she had taught and played with her from five years old – how she had devoted all her powers to attach and amuse her in health – and how nursed her though the various illnesses of childhood. A large debt of gratitude was owing here; but the intercourse of the last seven years, the equal footing and perfect nreserved which had soon followed Isabella's marriage on their being left to each other, was yet a dearer, tenderer recollection. It had been a friend and companion such as few possessed, intelligent, well-informed, useful, gentle, knowing all the ways of the family, interested in all its concerns, and peculiarly interested in herself, in every pleasure, every scheme of hers; – one to whom she could speak every thought as it arose, and who had such an affection for her as could never find fault.

Opening passages are always highly significant; this introductory piece gives a great deal of information to the reader about character, theme and tone. The preliminary statement which succinctly describes Emma's situation is unusual in itself for Austen. In all her other novels, the central characters are young marriageable females whose journey towards happy union is fraught with concern over their relative penury. However Emma is not only 'handsome' and 'clever' but, most significantly, 'rich'. She is an heir to the Hartfield fortunes and as such will not suffer the same concerns of the Bennett sisters in *Pride and Prejudice*, nor Eleanor and Marianne in *Sense and Sensibility*. Her financial independence is stated blandly without embellishment; it is to be noted, it is important, but taste forbids dwelling on the details. Thus Austen draws our attention to Emma's situation whilst placing the fact as apparently lesser in importance than her physical appearance or intelligence.

The listing of Emma's qualities appears to make her destined to suffer none of the painful quests for romantic happiness suffered by other Austen heroines. However, the narrative voice offers a tacit warning towards the dangers of a complacent attitude: Emma only 'seemed' to unite these blessings. There is more to be learned, it appears. Furthermore, by explaining that her past life had held nothing short of perfect contentment, there is the clear message that the course of the novel will present an end to this state of blissful happiness; that Emma's situation is to change for the worse. The reader is advised to avoid complacency; there is 'danger' ahead for Emma, danger which will apparently directly result from the circumstances of her present state.

In fact, the narrator alludes to the 'evils of Emma's situation' very clearly. For a young woman of intelligence to have received no firm guidance is not necessarily such a desirable state of affairs. Her father is indulgent and affectionate in the extreme. He can see no wrong in his daughter, and is not a man of sense or reason himself. Thus there can be no question of firm paternal guidance. Emma has likewise received little in the way of character-forming advice or restraint from her governess. In fact, her devotion to Miss Taylor appears to result largely from the latter's acquiescence to every whim and fancy of her charge. No adult in her circle offers any form of restraint, and to have such control over one's life from a very formative age is, the narrator warns, bound to cause negative results.

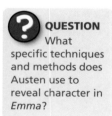

QUESTION
What specific techniques and methods does Austen use to reveal character in *Emma*?

She is very pointedly described as 'clever' rather than intelligent, thoughtful, reasoned – any of which terms would have a more complimentary, positive resonance. To be clever without reason is not necessarily a beneficial quality; the narrator is once again directing attention towards a quality in Emma that may cause problems. She is indeed clever, especially when observed alongside her father or Harriet, but her intelligence is unformed and lacking in focus and she has very little self-knowledge.

Emma's relationship with Miss Taylor is grounded in the fact of Emma having prominence. As Mr Knightley points out later on, Emma has never listened to advice from anyone, and it is presumably no fault of Miss Taylor's that she is unable to guide Emma towards the profitable and useful passage of her days. When Miss Taylor marries, the void left by her absence is bound to lead to trouble for Emma. Not only has she now no daily companion, but she has nothing to do; no distracting buffer to mask her indolence. It is this fact which leads her into the disastrous friendship with Harriet Smith; she uses Harriet for her own self-seeking motives and pays the consequences for this.

Emma's dominance in the household supersedes any influence of her elder sister. In spite of being the younger sister, she has a far closer relationship with Miss Taylor, and since Isabella's marriage has become the nominal only child of her father. When Isabella is introduced later on, it is apparent that such hints as to Emma's having the stronger character of the two sisters have their basis in truth. Isabella is a female version of her father: gentle, obsessed with health, very delicate and not particularly bright. One can only imagine that she faded into insignificance next to her vibrant little sister in their youth.

The theme of marriage is clearly foregrounded by the author in this introductory passage, thus marking its centrality to the plot of the novel as a whole. The story opens on the day of Miss Taylor's wedding to Mr Weston, highlighting for Emma how isolated she will become as a result of their marriage. Although Miss Taylor's situation has improved dramatically from this alliance, Emma cannot help but be conscious of the negative results for herself. The pursuit of, the search for, and the desirability of marriage, are prominent themes in all of Austen's work. In *Emma*, the pains and joys attached to such pursuit of happy union have prominent status. This is partly due to the novel being a romantic comedy, and thus adhering to classical tradition. From the earliest days of theatre, marriage was a central theme in the notion of comedy, and the main plot always involved a pair of lovers who would proceed on a journey towards their inevitable union. The novel is clearly exalting the 'romantic' in its celebration of marriage of unequal alliance: Miss Taylor is in her thirties, has no means or family titles, and yet is marrying a wealthy landowner. In spite of later preoccupations with equality of alliance, this marriage is approved of because of the equality of the people and the love they feel for each other, notwithstanding their apparent disparity.

> **? QUESTION**
> Discuss the various character's attitudes towards marriage in the novel.

Furthermore, Emma takes credit for the wedding between her governess and Mr Weston: an idea which is rooted in plot development. She believes herself to be responsible for the marriage taking place, in spite of suffering the consequences of her 'black morning's work'. The irony of this statement is that she, in taking little pleasure in the situation which she believes she has created, does not learn from the emotion she is suffering; if she had done so, she would be spared the self-inflicted pain later on.

Throughout the preliminary passage, the author takes a stance of third-person **omniscient narrator**, redolent with ironic commentary. Austen preferred this style, although she had dabbled with others in early work, particularly the **epistolary** form favoured by Richardson. However, third-person suits the maintenance of contemplative observation. It is through such a technique that the tone of ironic distance may be maintained; the reader is given gentle nudges and warnings without any judgement appearing to be passed. The worst that is claimed of Emma here is that she has the tendency to 'think a little too well of herself' – gentle criticism indeed, given the heights of arrogance of which she is capable. However, the narrator maintains at all times a distance from involvement in the form of any judgement, merely reporting events as they appear. There is an air of civility in the narrator's observations about Emma; an intelligence that we, as readers, will discover everything we need to see in our own terms and time.

TEXT 2 – CHAPTER 15 (PP. 101–2)

During the carriage-ride home from Randalls, Mr Elton seizes this moment to profess his hopes to Emma that she may return his affection for her. Coming as it does towards the end of Volume 1 of the novel, this passage is significant in that it highlights the results of Emma's meddling in the affairs of others when she ought to have more gainful employment. Although dreadfully awkward and painful for the main players, the passage affords a piece of high comedy for the reader. The authorial voice has made Mr Elton's intentions markedly clear to us from his first entrance in the novel, and it is just that Emma now suffers from her own lack of foresight.

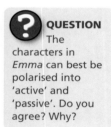

QUESTION
The characters in *Emma* can best be polarised into 'active' and 'passive'. Do you agree? Why?

'It is impossible for me to doubt any longer. You have made yourself too clear. Mr Elton, my astonishment is much beyond any thing I can express. After such behaviour, as I have witnessed during the last month, to Miss Smith – such attentions as I have been in the daily habit of observing – to be addressing me in this manner – this is an unsteadiness of character, indeed, which I had not supposed possible! Believe me, sir, I am far, very far, from gratified in being the object of such professions.'

'Good heaven!' cried Mr Elton, 'what can be the meaning of this? – Miss Smith! – I never thought of Miss Smith in the whole course of my existence – never paid her any attentions, but as your friend. If she has fancied otherwise, her own wishes have misled her, and I am very sorry – extremely sorry – But, Miss Smith, indeed! – Oh! Miss Woodhouse! Who can think of Miss Smith, when Miss Woodhouse is near! No, upon my honour, there is no unsteadiness of character. I have thought only of you. I protest against having paid the smallest attention to any one else. Every thing that I have said or done, for many weeks past, has been with the sole view of marking my adoration of yourself. You cannot really, seriously, doubt it. No! – (in an accent meant to be insinuating) – I am sure you have seen and understood me.'

It would be impossible to say what Emma felt, on hearing this – which of all her unpleasant sensations was uppermost. She was too completely overpowered to be immediately able to reply: and two moments of silence being ample encouragement for Mr Elton's sanguine state of mind, he tried to take her hand again, as he joyously exclaimed –

'Charming Miss Woodhouse! Allow me to interpret this interesting silence. It confesses that you have long understood me.'

'No, sir,' cried Emma, 'it confesses no such thing. So far from having long understood you, I have been in a most complete error with respect to your views, till this moment. As to myself, I am very sorry that you should have been giving way to any feelings – Nothing could be farther from my wishes – your attachment to my friend Harriet – your pursuit of her, (pursuit, it appeared,) gave me great pleasure, and I have been very earnestly wishing you success: but had I supposed that she were not your attraction to Hartfield, I should certainly have thought you judged ill in making your visits so frequent. Am I to believe that you have never sought to recommend yourself particularly to Miss Smith? – that you have never thought seriously of her?'

'Never, madam, 'cried he, affronted in his turn: 'never, I assure you. *I* think seriously of Miss Smith!- Miss Smith is a very good sort of girl, and I should be happy to see her respectably settled. I wish her extremely well: and, no doubt, there are men who might not object to – Every body has their level: but as for

myself, I am not, I think, quite so much at a loss. I need not so
totally despair of an equal alliance, as to be addressing myself to
Miss Smith! – No, madam, my visit to Hartfield have been for
yourself only; and the encouragement I received' –

'Encouragement! – I give you encouragement! – sir, you have
been entirely mistaken in supposing it. I have seen you only as
the admirer of my friend. In no other light could you have been
more to me than a common acquaintance. I am exceedingly
sorry: but it is well that the mistake ends where it does. Had the
same behaviour continued, Miss Smith might have been led into
a misconception of your views, not being aware, probably, any
more than myself, of the very great inequality which you are so
sensible of. But, as it is, the disappointment is singe, and, I trust,
will not be lasting. I have no thoughts of matrimony at present.'

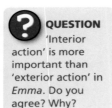

The characters are conveniently placed for this exchange. The
carriage is small, private and enclosed; it affords no possibility of
easy escape for either participant. Thus both Emma and Mr Elton
are trapped together for the duration of the journey home; although
a distance of no more than a mile, the time together appears
interminable. Mr Elton has presumably seized his moment
deliberately for exactly that reason, having confidently assumed that
Emma's response would be favourable. Little does he suspect that
his proposal should lead to such mortification for both parties.

His confidence in Emma's affection for him shakes her to her very
core. However, in spite of his arrogance in presuming so far, he
speaks honestly and gives a faithful report of how the preceding
weeks have appeared to him to be encouragement of his affection
for Emma alone. The truth of his statements does nothing to
assuage Emma's mortification as the overpowering clarity of her
mistake is brought home to her.

Although the reader has been given plenty of prior opportunity to
observe Emma's striking ability to interpret events and behaviour in
her own misguided way, this passage of conversation crystallises her
mistake. By using direct speech and removing the narrative voice,
the author uses the technique of foregrounding to display how far
Emma can be misguided. Nothing comes between reader and

characters here; the extent of their conversation is related whole and without dilution. In fact, no commentary from the narrator is necessary to magnify the **irony** inherent within this passage. For example, Emma's assertion that she has been 'in the daily habit of observing' Mr Elton's attentions to Harriet, the irony of which is remarkably clear, highlights the ridiculous nature of her criticism of his 'unsteadiness of character'. Whatever else he may be, Mr Elton is far from unsteady in his devotion. He has made his intentions plain and clear from the outset, and it is simply Emma's blindness which has allowed her to miss his aim completely.

Emma struggles to make sense of this apparent shift in circumstance; so far from what she believed to be the truth. Uppermost in her mind is the realisation that it is her own mistake which has led to this appalling situation. Divided between two very unpleasant emotions – insulted that Mr Elton could presume to raise his sights to her, and mortified that her blinkered interference has caused such confusion – she resists facing the truth and persists with her idea that he is, in fact, in love with Harriet. This struggle is not aided by his comment that Harriet's 'own wishes have misled her'; in fact it is Emma, and not Harriet, who is completely to blame and Emma knows it. She attempts to deflect attention from her own part in the mistake with choice of terms such as 'witness', 'observing', and 'appeared'; all of which are designed to place her at one remove rather than be known as the main perpetrator. She further states that she has 'been earnestly wishing you success', which, although true, is not a just account of her meddling interference in their lives.

As the reality of the situation makes itself clear, Emma begins to realise that by her own actions, Mr Elton has received encouragement to pay attention to her; furthermore, to believe that she returns his affection. Their respective sense of social standing is pronounced here; Mr Elton is an ambitious, worldly man who thinks well of himself and sees nothing wrong with compounding his sense of himself as a gentleman by making an alliance with Emma Woodhouse. Mr Knightley has already warned Emma of this trait in Mr Elton, but she chose to ignore the advice. He is grossly insulted that his name could ever be romantically linked with someone such as Harriet; 'everybody has their level'.

QUESTION
Discuss the different kinds of irony in *Emma*, what examples can you find to support your ideas?

Emma is equally affronted. Mr Elton's comment that he 'need not so totally despair of an equal alliance' implies that he feels himself on equal social terms with herself. Far from being his equal, she feels that she is his social superior and is insulted that he dare consider her in marriageable terms. This sense of social snobbery runs throughout the novel, and can be partly attributed to Emma's immaturity in that she struggles to value people for who they are rather than what their status represents. She learns from Mr Knightley to see value where it is due, and comes in time to admit her mistake. However at this moment, she is displaying a highly ironic duality of belief. Whilst on the one hand feeling insulted that Mr Elton should dare to attempt to breach the chasm she perceives between their respective social states – he was 'quite the gentleman… and without low connections; at the same time not of any family that could fairly object to the doubtful birth of Harriet' (Ch. 4, p. 27) – she refuses to allow that such disparity exists between himself and Harriet; 'not being aware, probably, any more than myself, of the very great inequality which you are so sensible of'.

Although the reader is allowed in part to sympathise with Mr Elton's situation here, resulting as it does from no real fault of his own other than ambition, his arrogance and pride is fully highlighted. He is completely convinced of Emma's affection for him; in spite of the apparent encouragement he has received, there is a level of arrogance which makes him just as liable to misjudgement as Emma is. The 'insinuating' tone he adopts feels as fawning and distasteful to the reader as it does to Emma. His interpretation of her silence as tacit acceptance of his proposal shows that he has not listened to a word she has said, and is pursuing his own aims relentlessly. When reduced to angry remonstrance by the idea that he could ever be considered as a match for Harriet, he struggles aloud to come to terms with what he is hearing. This battle is displayed through broken, unfinished sentences linked by a series of dashes, markedly different to the romantic, calculating prose he has previously adopted. His arrogant presumption of status, unmasked by temper, shows his true nature. He is a colossal snob of the worst sort; his desire to make a match with a wealthy woman has led to him desiring Emma to fulfil that function. As a clergyman he would not be well off; this type of living was normally reserved for second sons, as the first-born would inherit any family titles and land.

Thus, although comfortable, Mr Elton clearly desires to gain additional social status by marrying 'well'. The spiritual aspect of his profession has relatively little importance; he has taken the living primarily as a means to support himself.

Overall this passage displays very clearly how both characters have misunderstood themselves and each other, and is significant in several ways. It teaches Emma her first lesson in the dangers attached to meddling with other people's lives. It forms the dramatic crisis to the events in Volume 1, thus ending that part of the narrative whilst clarifying the themes of social status and mistaken motivation. It is a perfect opportunity for Emma to learn a lesson, and for the reader to see the results of her indolence, although the tone here is ironic and comic rather than grave.

TEXT 3 – CHAPTER 38 (PP. 244–5)

> **QUESTION**
> What are the patterns of dramatic tension in the novel?

The evening of the ball at the Crown is significant in that much of the intrigue between the central characters is beginning to gain momentum. Emma feels herself to have a pivotal role and yet her mistaken assumptions regarding the feelings of herself and others is highlighted very notably, and publicly, here. This passage marks the similarity between herself and Mrs Elton very clearly; both believing themselves first in prominence.

'Nobody can think less of dress in general than I do – but upon such an occasion as this, when everybody's eyes are so much upon me, and in compliment to the Westons – who I have no doubt are giving this ball chiefly to do me honour – I would not wish to be inferior to others. And I see very few pearls in the room except mine. – So Frank Churchill is a capital dancer, I understand. – We shall see if our styles suit. – A fine young man certainly is Frank Churchill. I like him very well.'

At this moment Frank began talking so vigorously, that Emma could not but imagine he had overheard his own praises, and did not want to hear more; – and the voices of the ladies were drowned for a while, till another suspension brought Mrs Elton's tones again distinctly forward. – Mr Elton had just joined them, and his wife was exclaiming,

'Oh! You have found us out at last, have you, in our seclusion? – I was this moment telling Jane, I thought you would begin to be impatient for tidings of us.'

'Jane!' – repeated Frank Churchill, with a look of surprise and displeasure. – 'That is easy – but Miss Fairfax does not disapprove it, I suppose.'

'How do you like Mrs Elton?' said Emma in a whisper.

'Not at all.'

'You are ungrateful'.

'Ungrateful!' – What do you mean?' Then changing from a frown to a smile – 'No, do not tell me – I do not want to know what you mean. – Where is my father? – When are we to begin dancing?'

Emma could hardly understand him; he seemed in an odd humour. He walked off to find his father, but was quickly back again with both Mr and Mrs Weston. He had met them in a little perplexity, which must be laid before Emma. It had just occurred to Mrs Weston that Mrs Elton must be asked to begin the ball; that she would expect it; which interfered with all their wishes of giving Emma that distinction. – Emma heard the sad truth with fortitude.

'And what are we to do for a proper partner for her?' said Mr Weston. 'She will think Frank ought to ask her.'

Frank turned instantly to Emma, to claim her former promise; and boasted himself an engaged man, which his father looked his most perfect approbation of – and then it appeared that Mrs Weston was wanting *him* to dance with Mrs Elton himself, and that their business to help to persuade him into it, which was done pretty soon. – Mr Weston and Mrs Elton led the way, Mr Frank Churchill and Miss Woodhouse followed. Emma must submit to stand second to Mrs Elton, though she had always considered the ball as peculiarly for her. It was almost enough to make her think of marrying.

Mrs Elton had undoubtedly the advantage, at this time, in vanity completely gratified; for though she had intended to begin with Frank Churchill, she could not lose by the change. Mr Weston might be his son's superior. – In spite of this little rub, however, Emma was smiling with enjoyment, delighted to see the respectable length of the set as it was forming, and to feel that she had so many hours of unusual festivity before her. – She was more disturbed by Mr Knightley's not dancing, than by any thing else. – There he was, among the standers-by, where he ought not to be; he ought to be dancing, – not classing himself with the husbands, and fathers, and whist-players, who were pretending to feel an interest in the dance till their rubbers were made up, – so young he looked!'

Mrs Elton could in fact be claimed to be a caricature of Emma's worst tendencies towards arrogant presumption. By the evening of the ball she has not only begun to snub Emma very obviously, but has claimed Jane Fairfax as her especial friend. It is to Jane that she addresses her opening remarks, once she has successfully drawn her aside for private conversation. This action is very rude and presumptuous, especially during a social occasion, but Mrs Elton has already shown herself to have few genuine social graces. The narrator refers to Jane's patience during this exchange, clearly implying that this virtue is necessary when engaged in conversation with Mrs Elton.

Her complimentary remarks to Jane are designed for nothing more than to have them returned in kind; Jane's gracious acceptance of her compliments does not satisfy her need to be flattered and she has to drop flagrant hints in order to receive her share. The narrator withdraws from reported speech in the first paragraph, allowing Mrs Elton a passage of direct speech which highlights her conceited air of self-satisfaction. She uses the personal pronoun nine times in this paragraph alone, referring every comment and observation back towards herself and thus accentuating her self-absorption. Her statement that she would 'not wish to be inferior to others' is an **ironically** honest statement; she consistently displays this need to be more important than anyone else and revels in her prominent social status as bride. Part of her disapproval of Emma stems from jealousy that the heiress of Hartfield has more status than she does.

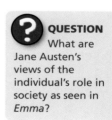

QUESTION
What are Jane Austen's views of the individual's role in society as seen in *Emma*?

When later in the novel she is discussing plans for the picnic at Donwell Abbey, she is flustered into panic at Mr Knightley's assertion that there may be another lady to whom she must defer.

Emma and Frank are placed to overhear this conversation, and Emma mistakes his quietness with her for 'thoughtfulness' when in fact he is completely focussed upon Jane and is straining to catch every word of hers. However, when the conversation turns to complimenting him, he remembers himself. Emma is intelligent enough to notice this, although she misunderstands the motive; in fact Frank has been jolted into recognising how his behaviour may appear and is at once on his guard to disguise any hints of feeling for Jane. Nevertheless, he is sure enough by this point that Emma has guessed the truth of the affair, and alludes to this when Emma refers to his being 'ungrateful' in his disapproval of Mrs Elton. She means by this that she is aware that he has overheard that lady's complimentary remarks about him; he, however, assumes she is referring to Mrs Elton's friendship with Jane, and stops her before she can say more. If Emma had been a little less self-absorbed, she would have noticed Frank's disapproval of Mrs Elton's use of 'Jane' rather than 'Miss Fairfax'; he is right to feel that such use is overfamiliar and presumptuous, but appears rather too disapproving for someone completely disinterested.

Still struggling to understand Frank's preoccupied mood, Emma is gratified at his insistence that he claim the first dance with her. However, recognising that Mrs Elton should be granted the honour of opening the dancing sits uncomfortably with her. The narrator blandly reports Emma's notion that the ball was for her; placed alongside Mrs Elton's remark that the ball is 'chiefly to do me honour'. The irony of both women, in their arrogance, wishing to be first in prominence, highlights the similarity between them.

The author shifts easily between narrative modes in this passage. When reporting on how the dancing was begun, the use of formal nomenclature is resonant of **reportage** technique; a disinterested observer giving an account of the evening at The Crown. This is swiftly followed by a lovely piece of wit, in the reported comment about Emma's distaste at being second; 'it was almost enough to make her think of marrying'. However, Emma's comment has a slight sense of self-mockery attached to it; Emma is far more aware than Mrs Elton of her desire to be important and has the ability to laugh at herself, and thus is less open to censure.

Emma is in her element on the dance floor, but her contentment is not complete. She is constantly distracted by observing Mr Knightley; wanting him to look at her, wishing he would dance, being favourably impressed by his youthful appearance and graceful movements. It never crosses her mind to analyse this tendency of hers to be so aware of him. Emma's state of mind at this point is a strange mixture of mistaken assumptions and quick judgement. Her affection for Mr Knightley is growing into love without her knowledge; in spite of being on the dance floor with the man she believes herself to be destined for, her whole attention is taken up with Mr Knightley.

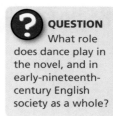

QUESTION
What role does dance play in the novel, and in early-nineteenth-century English society as a whole?

PART THREE

CRITICAL APPROACHES

CHARACTERISATION

Jane Austen employs a distinctive narrative technique in all her novels. The reader is invited to observe the central character not merely through the **omniscient narrator**, and the plot and structure, but through parallels between the heroine and other characters who either resemble her or display points of dissimilarity. Thus, knowledge of those around Emma allows the reader to form a clearer picture of her own behaviour and moral nature.

EMMA WOODHOUSE

Emma is young, beautiful, rich and clever. The narrator informs us very pointedly, in the opening sentence, of her merits. However even here there is **irony**. The narrator, although omniscient, places the observational stance alongside Emma throughout the novel, allowing the reader to observe primarily through her eyes. When the narrator steps back, the distance created between the reader's observation, and what Emma understands, is the ironic distance. Thus, we are invited to assume that this opening summary of the heroine's virtues is, in fact, her own estimation of herself.

Emma is remarkably independent for one so young. Although her father is living, he is little more than a dependent child in his hold over his daughter; she loves and cares for him but there is no doubt that she rules the household. She has been without a mother for many years, and Miss Taylor's office was more friend and confidant than strict governess. She is immensely wealthy, thus has no need to marry for fortune. She is used to having her own way and is first in Highbury society; in fact, the only checking mechanism she has ever known is the kind voice of reason offered by Mr Knightley. She is loved and admired by everyone around her.

Furthermore, Emma is very intelligent. She is a sound judge of character, as witnessed time and again in her accurate summation of those she meets, as well as her choice of those she holds dear. There is no doubt that Mr Knightley and Mrs Weston, as her closest friends, are people of great worth and moral kindness. Her dislike

CONTEXT

As a member of the landed gentry, Emma's family had a direct responsibility for the welfare of those people living on her family's estate.

of Mr and Mrs Elton is reasonable, as are her suspicions regarding Frank Churchill. She is cuttingly aware of Harriet's lack of intelligence, to the point of contempt for her intellectual fibre.

In the face of the undeniable virtues of character and situation, her faults are even more palpable and difficult to avoid. The largest of these is her unspeakable arrogance: the flaw in her nature which drives her need to interfere with the lives of others and act badly, in her need to remain supreme in the eyes of everyone around her. It is this arrogance which uses her friends' feelings for her own amusement: they become pawns in her romantic games. It is inevitable, and with a strong sense of **poetic justice**, that she unwittingly becomes a pawn in the same kind of game herself. The second, but by no means less important flaw, is her lack of humility; her belief that financial and societal status are their own key to a primary position in society.

> **CONTEXT**
>
> For a young woman of Emma's social standing, drawing would be one of the skills taught by her governess. It was seen as an appropriate pursuit for a lady and would be taught along with music, French and sewing.

However, Austen clearly wants the reader to see, as Mr Knightley does, that Emma is redeemable. Her worthier character traits are not stated overtly at the start of the novel, presumably because Emma herself does not recognise them as valuable. One of them is displayed very obviously however, in the passage where she visits a sick local family. 'Emma was very compassionate; and the distresses of the poor were as sure of relief from her personal attention and kindness, her counsel and her patience, as from her purse' (Ch. 10, p. 68). This same compassion is consistently demonstrated by her patience towards her father.

Overriding all other considerations as to Emma's likeability is that she also learns her lessons: albeit slowly. The pain she feels at knowing her blunders are the cause of Harriet's suffering is genuine and heartfelt. Once her own games are practised upon herself and she learns at first hand the dangers of such self-serving interference, her growth into self-knowledge and humility is rapid and genuine. Luckily, there are no lasting negative consequences to her actions and it is enough that she has, by the end of the novel, matured sufficiently to be worthy of Mr Knightley's love.

Of the other characters in the novel, there are three in particular whose function it is to demonstrate parallels to, or differences from, Emma herself. The first of these is Mrs Elton.

MRS ELTON

Mrs Elton is an outrageous character. Although she is primarily a comic figure, she does not engender the gentle comedy offered by Miss Bates; Mrs Elton is harsh, brash and unbelievably arrogant; causing the reader to cringe with amused embarrassment at her behaviour.

She enters the novel to spearhead the pride and arrogance of her new husband. His speedy exit was occasioned by a curt, definite refusal of marriage from Emma; incensed by his pride in daring to raise his hopes to her. It is inevitable that he, as a result of his natural inflated sense of his own worth and desire to prove Emma unequal to him, would present a manifestation of that very pride which is so much a theme of the novel, and a comic device for the author.

QUESTION
Examine the character functions of Mrs Elton and Jane Fairfax as foils to Emma.

Relieved to be married at last, and to a gentleman with his own 'living', Mrs Elton is determined to make herself first in Highbury society. Not content with the fuss and notice naturally accorded a new bride, she immediately desires to ingratiate herself with Emma as first lady of Highbury society. She is boastful and rude, constantly comparing everybody and everything to her brother-in-law's circle; the only claim to good society she knows. When she turns against Emma, her next action is to declare herself superior by becoming the patroness of Jane Fairfax. Her desire to take over every social event in Highbury is met with initial polite acquiescence, although it is not long before her manner begins to wear thin. Her overfamiliarity, lack of taste and flamboyant external show mark her as a woman who needs everyone to know how special and important she is. Her arrogance is ridiculous and designed for humour.

However, the character of Mrs Elton does not merely serve as a comic device, but as a characterisation technique. Her arrogance, her patronage of Jane Fairfax, her complete insensibility to her effect on those around her, are all criticisms which may justly be placed at Emma's door. Emma patronises Harriet in the same way; she takes over Harriet's life for her own purposes with little scruple. Furthermore, Mrs Elton's decision to 'help' Jane Fairfax keenly highlights how remiss Emma has been to Jane. Emma is extremely arrogant, in fact she is jealous of Mrs Elton's temporary status; 'Emma must submit to stand second to Mrs Elton, though she had always considered the ball as peculiarly for her. It was almost enough to make her think of marrying' (Ch. 38, p. 245). In fact, Mrs Elton is a caricature of Emma; the natural extension of her negative qualities taken to an extreme. Emma having far more intelligence and taste than Mrs Elton, only serves to make her own behaviour far less justifiable.

JANE FAIRFAX

Using the same principle, Jane Fairfax presents the other end of the spectrum to Mrs Elton; the other logical extension of Emma, but this time of her best qualities. Indeed, Mr Knightley's approbation of Jane demonstrates his estimation of the qualities which she and Emma share, and explain why he, in better knowledge of Emma's best side, is determined to improve and extend them in her.

Jane benefits from similar beauty, grace and sense. She is a gentleman's daughter, brought up as a lady with all the advantages afforded a lady. She is very well educated and has taken full advantage of that education. Emma is palpably reminded of her own lack of industry whenever the two are together and comparisons are drawn between their relative accomplishments on the piano.

> **CONTEXT**
>
> For the story of another young woman forced into the position of governess, read *Jane Eyre* by Charlotte Brontë.

In every respect it is expected that the two women be friends; however Emma, who cannot suffer equal comparison, avoids this whenever she can, blaming Jane's coldness and 'reserve' (Ch. 20, p. 125) for their lack of closeness. Jane's nature is very different to Emma's; she is quiet in company whereas Emma tends to be sociable and outgoing. Furthermore, Jane has a very different fate in store for her than Emma's as lady of the manor; she is destined to be a governess. Thus, although equal and even superior in some respects to Emma, she is materially inferior. Emma would find it very painful to be constantly in the company of one who presents a striking reminder of her own failings. Her need to be superior, which is based very much like Mrs Elton's on the shaky foundations of birthright and social status, will not tolerate proximity to Jane Fairfax.

Jane's function in the novel as a character is minimal. She is more important as an element in the plot device designed to draw Emma

CHECK THE NET

Search the internet for the Brontë sisters, who had to become governesses to support themselves.

into exactly the kind of intrigue which she practises on others. Her function as character reflection is far more significant. It is therefore reasonable that Emma finds it impossible to reconcile herself to Jane until she has dealt with those negative aspects of her own personality which impede her from hitherto forming a friendship with her.

MISS BATES

The third, but by no means least, comparative character is that of Miss Bates. Harriet is the first to light unwittingly on the potential comparison between her and Emma – much to the latter's dismay. Miss Bates is a harmless spinster, the aunt of Jane Fairfax, regarded warmly by everyone for her sweet temper and kindness. However, she is undeniably very tedious company indeed due to her complete inability to hold her own tongue. Her incessant stream of mindless chatter dominates wherever she goes and Emma is not the only person to find it tiresome.

However, Miss Bates' place in society is an uneasy alliance for Emma between that of unmarried woman and friendly neighbour. She is treated with warm regard because of her kind nature and her lack of wealth. Harriet points out that Emma's decision to never marry will mean her ending 'an old maid at last, like Miss Bates!' (Ch. 10, p. 67). Emma roundly refutes this idea, having a clear idea of her days being filled with industry, kind offices to those around her and benign charity work. But she would have none of the warmth and affection offered to Miss Bates, and it is her inability to see the merits of that lady's situation which once again shows her lack of insight.

Furthermore, Miss Bates is the locus of one of the most painful passages in the novel; the stunning example of Emma's high-handed cruelty at Box Hill. This instance is highly significant as it occasions the first real tears we have seen Emma shed; the shock of her words and their effect on Mr Knightley cause her genuine pain and a concrete desire to put right the wrong she has done. This seemingly tiny incident also **epitomises** the main theme of the novel; the potential harm done to human feelings by playing games. Miss Bates is a character to be borne with, sympathised with, smiled at, but her inferior status and very kind heart means that unkindness to her is unpardonable.

MR KNIGHTLEY

Mr Knightley is surely the most decent, kind and honourable of Austen's heroes. He is an old established friend of the family, linked through land-ownership as well as family ties. He has watched Emma grow from a baby and she considers him as a sort of benevolent uncle. He represents a paternal office far more effectively than her own father; his gentle, well-meant but firm insistence on putting her right and warning her from wrong-doing are a constant guide and check to her character.

In fact, Austen so clearly approves of Mr Knightley that he is virtually never wrong. He shows clarity and insight in his judgement of Mr Elton, Mrs Elton and Frank Churchill. He rightly suspects Emma of interfering in Harriet's affections, and asserts that 'You have been no friend to Harriet Smith, Emma' (Ch. 8, p. 49). He is courtesy itself to Harriet at the ball when Mr Elton so blatantly snubs her, and then guesses at the reason behind such rudeness. He remains determined to act as Emma's friend even when his own feelings are severely tested through Emma and Frank's open flirtation. The delightful conversation between himself and Miss Bates through her open window is testament to how far his own brusqueness can be tempered with gentleness and courtesy.

His guarded jealousy of Frank Churchill, combined with natural suspicion and disapproval of the young man's selfishness, manifests itself in an unwillingness to see any good in the man. However, even here he can be forgiven and understood. Overall, he is a wonderful hero for Emma, and his own good taste and sense enables the reader to trust his judgement with regard to his choice of bride.

QUESTION
Frank Churchill and Mr Knightley represent two different sets of understanding of manhood. Describe the values that each character represents and explain how the novel judges these values.

FRANK CHURCHILL

Frank Churchill is the dashing young hero; the obvious partner for the heroine as judged by narrative protocol, and certainly by Emma, Mr Weston and Mrs Weston. Socially and financially equal, with similar claims of birthright and place in their families, the match is an apparent foregone conclusion even before Frank has entered the novel.

However, Frank's arrival is preceded by a sense of unease voiced by Mr Knightley and privately supported by Emma herself. He has never, in twenty three years, paid his father a visit to his home at Randalls. What is more, Mr Weston's recent marriage would surely demand that the son pay his respects to his father's new wife. Frank promises visits often, but does not appear in fact until well into Volume II.

By entering into a secret engagement with Jane Fairfax he places her honour as well as her situation in life in great difficulty. The only inevitable conclusion to such an arrangement would be pain to the lady; it is Frank's good fortune that his irascible aunt dies and leaves him free to marry whom he wishes, his uncle being no match for his own will.

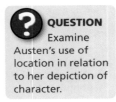

QUESTION
Examine Austen's use of location in relation to her depiction of character.

Frank is Emma's male counterpart in situation as well as character. Both have doting fathers who see no fault in them. Both behave very selfishly, using others to their own advantage. Both are very young and inexperienced. They play games with the feelings of others, to the extent that their own happiness is jeopardised as a result. Emma, in her eventual wisdom, points this out to Frank; 'I think there is a little likeness between us...If not in our dispositions, there is a likeness in our destiny; the destiny which bids fair to connect us with two characters to much superior to our own' (Ch. 54, pp. 362–3).

HARRIET SMITH

Poor Harriet. Harriet Smith is a 'parlour-boarder' (Ch. 3, p. 18) at a local girls' boarding school run by an old friend of Mr Woodhouse, Mrs Goddard. Harriet is first noticed, unluckily for her, by Emma just after Miss Taylor's wedding has left her bereft of company and casting around for something to do. In spite of all Miss Taylor and Mr Knightley's efforts to encourage her to use her time judiciously for self-improvement, Emma decides that the best use of her time, and the best distraction from idleness, will be to make a lady out of Harriet Smith.

Having noticed her for her pretty face, Emma quickly (and very conveniently for herself) decides that such a face can only be the product of noble birth. Harriet's shady past as 'the natural daughter of somebody' (Ch. 3, p. 18) would be a natural bar to friendship under normal circumstances, therefore Emma makes expedient use of fancy to create a romantic aristocratic birthright for her friend.

Of course Harriet turns out to be the daughter of a tradesman: not fitting company or social standing for Emma at all. Harriet is a very sweet, simple girl but extremely dull and stupid. Emma is stunned by her reaction to the riddle sent by Mr Elton on the word 'Courtship' – 'I never saw anything so hard. Is it kingdom?...Can it be Neptune? Or a trident? Or a mermaid? Or a shark? Oh, no! shark is only one syllable. It must be very clever...' (Ch. 9, pp. 56–7).

However, even she proves to be more in charge of her own heart than Emma is: 'the fact was, as Emma could now acknowledge, that Harriet had always liked Robert Martin' (Ch. 55, p. 365). Although not strong enough to withstand Emma's influence when the two of them are together, she remains true to her first and only love and accepts him as soon as he gives her opportunity.

MR WOODHOUSE

Emma's father commands high status amongst Highbury society. He is one of the oldest residents, which in itself demands respect. More importantly, he is the richest man in the area, which goes much further towards explaining the deference with which he is treated.

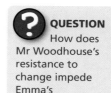

QUESTION
How does Mr Woodhouse's resistance to change impede Emma's development into adulthood?

However, he is a man of little sense or intelligence. His obsession with health is a constant source of worry for him, and irritation for everyone else. He is fussed over, protected and cosseted by everyone, especially Emma, who treats him very kindly indeed given how demanding he clearly is.

He is also a very selfish man who is 'never able to suppose that other people could feel differently from himself' (Ch. 1, p. 7). This selfishness is especially marked in the face of such laudable disinterested kindness manifested by Mrs Weston and Mr Knightley in particular, but also praised in Miss Bates and Jane Fairfax. It seems strange that if selflessness is such a highly prized character trait, Mr Woodhouse's total self-centredness does not make him a less sympathetic character.

His selfishness is not dangerous or hurtful however; he commands the deference of his family and associates by dint of age and status, and is accorded no more than his due. If he were a cruel man then he would no doubt receive less sympathetic treatment; as it is, he is merely a figure provoking gentle fun.

MR ELTON

Mr Elton is very far from being the self-deprecating embodiment of Christian virtue one would expect in a man of the cloth. He has taken the option open to second sons of gentlemen, whose first-born would take over the family estate; he has purchased a 'living' of parish and vicarage at Highbury.

Mr Elton thinks very highly of himself and intends to fare very well in marriage. He sets his sights on Emma as the first lady of consequence in Highbury, never considering for a moment that she may be insulted by this. His behaviour towards Emma prior to his hilarious proposal can only be described as 'toadying' in the extreme. Once his pride has been hurt, he is speedy in retreat and only returns home (and to his abandoned parishioners) when he has acquired a bride. His choice of wife itself says a great deal about his own character.

Appearing compliant and friendly to those around him, this can quickly be seen to be merely ingratiating himself to advance his own position in society. His behaviour towards Harriet at the ball in collusion with his wife and accompanied by 'smiles of high glee' (Ch. 38, p. 247) serve to mark him as anything but a Christian, or a gentleman in the true sense.

MRS WESTON

Mrs Weston is a gentle, kind woman who loves everyone around her. She appears to have a great deal of sensitivity and common sense, and is furthermore served by a natural propensity to be happy.

Her marriage to a gentleman of local consequence is fortunate for her, taking her from relatively minor status as governess into settled, respectable marital comfort. Her marriage is clearly a happy one and her husband loves her dearly.

Mrs Weston's only flaw is a tendency to be blind to fault in others. She has never guided Emma as well as she could, allowing Emma's

? QUESTION
Discuss how your opinion of Mr Elton changes after he reveals his indifference to Harriet and his desire to marry Emma.

strong will to dominate even from her youth. She remains insensible to Emma's faults now, and thus is not the best judge of character for her. Furthermore, she remains constantly loyal to Frank Churchill and demands that Emma not judge him too harshly.

MR WESTON

Mr Weston is the life and soul of the party; always ready to be cheerful, to entertain friends and to host parties, much to the disapproval of the rather taciturn John Knightley. He is well off, so that he is able to marry Emma's governess who has no dowry.

He is completely obsessed by his son and can see no fault in him whatsoever. Although Emma has very warm feelings for him, she finds his lack of discernment somewhat frustrating. His open nature and inability to keep a secret are well known, and even counted upon when Emma and Mr Knightley want to spread the news of their engagement.

THEMES

SELFLESSNESS

The virtue of self-denial is much lauded in *Emma*. Humility, not merely self-deprecating humbleness but true self-knowledge is initially lacking in Emma's nature; and her journey towards mature humility marks her path into adulthood.

The most admirable characters in the book are in great measure admired for their selflessness. Miss Bates, for all her irritating chatter, is tolerated and respected for her decent, heartfelt desire to see good in others at all times and gratitude for the kindness of her friends. Jane Fairfax tolerates a great deal and is never seen to complain. Mrs Weston refuses to see any other motive but kindness in everyone, and is eminently forgiving.

Although such selflessness can manifest itself as naïve, blinkered innocence, it is perceived to be preferable to the inflated arrogance of Mr and Mrs Elton, and even the selfishness of Emma and Frank Churchill. Emma and Frank have the fact of their youth on their side; to a certain extent their selfishness is tolerated and they are allowed the luxury of growth into maturity by knowledge and acceptance of their errors. They are far more sympathetic characters than the Eltons, who have none of the formers' excuses for their behaviour and attitudes.

Emma's selfishness is partly circumstantial: 'The real evils indeed of Emma's situation were the power of having rather too much her own way' (Ch. 1, p. 5), due to lack of guidance in her youth. Furthermore, Emma demonstrates the mediating quality of selflessness in her devotion to her father, which bodes well for her future self being far less selfish all round. Her selfishness is mediated by constant care for the feelings of those she cares for, and ultimately in her good taste in choosing Mr Knightley for her lover. Frank also is shown to have taste and thoughtfulness in his choice of a wife, which goes a fair way to excuse the selfishly extravagant behaviour of his youth and thoughtlessness towards his father.

> **CONTEXT**
>
> Emma struggles to shed her vanity and her fear of confronting her own feelings, both of which cause her to misunderstand those around her and to meddle harmfully in the lives of others.

Mr Woodhouse is painted as a mildly ridiculous character; his selfishness is described by the narrator as 'gentle' (Ch. 1, p. 7) rather than dangerous and, although irritating, his status, years and semi-invalid status require a level of tolerance towards his behaviour not deserved by others. His own selfishness is in fact used against him to promote the happiness of others. Emma is grateful to the thieves who raid her friend's chicken house, thereby giving her a perfect excuse with her father when persuading him that her marriage will increase his personal safety. As this action does nothing but ensure good results to all who benefit from it, the narrator is, although not condoning, far from condemning Mr Woodhouse for his tendencies.

As testament to the utter supremacy of selflessness as a virtue, Mr Knightley, ever the vanguard of good judgement and decent behaviour, places his own comfort and happiness below that of Emma and Mr Woodhouse by sacrificing the peace and tranquillity of his own home and moving to Hartfield.

SOCIETAL STRUCTURES

Emma is firmly rooted in **Augustan** notions of social hierarchy: permanent, virtually impermeable and quintessentially English.

From royalty down, society was governed by strict rules of adherence to rank and place. One might dabble one's toes in the occasional social mixture, but to tread further than this – especially through marriage – was severely frowned upon. However, Austen was writing at the beginning of the nineteenth century; the century which saw the most dramatic upheaval in social structures and the move away from baronial organisation of power. The 'middle class' – that is, the class of landowners and work-force owners, were beginning to make their mark and carve a place in society, and *Emma* is concerned with the immense social snobbery of this 'new' class. In fact, the novel can be seen as a social satire poking fun at this stratum of society, which was the most concerned with class and status and the least confident of its own social position.

Mr Woodhouse and Mr Knightley, as substantial landowners, are first in prominence. Furthermore, their landownership is hereditary; their families have owned and lived on the same estates for generations. This marks them as gentlemen from England's historical period of feudalism. They are 'lords of the manor', if not actual landed gentry. High rank in society was dictated more by family history than current wealth. Hereditary wealth was perceived as infinitely superior to recently earned, 'new money'. One of Emma's objections to Mrs Elton is her self-inflated ideas of social status: 'She brought no name, no blood, no alliance. Miss Hawkins was the youngest of two daughters of a Bristol-merchant' (Ch. 22, p. 138).

Mr Weston, although not historically a landowner, stems from a 'good' or well-established family. His claim to high social status is marked by having worked hard, in a series of respectable and profitable ventures, finally to secure a reasonable estate himself. Prior to this he was an army officer, the position most favoured by second or third sons of gentlemen, who, because not first-born, would not inherit their father's estate.

Frank Churchill, as his son, is entitled to the same social position as his father. Frank also benefits from the familial ties to his late mother's family; another high-ranking, well-established name. As first and only son, he will inherit his father's estate, presumably in addition to being heir of the Churchill fortune.

 CHECK THE NET
Use a comprehensive online encyclopedia such as http://en. wikipedia.org to search for 'Industrial Revolution' with a history of how the rise of the manufacturing industry in Great Britain impacted upon society in the eighteenth and nineteenth centuries.

Society reinforced its own structures through tacit disapproval of the rise in financial – and social – status of 'new money'. Increases in international trading and the beginnings of the Industrial Revolution saw a rise of the merchant classes during this period of English history. With the increase in trade wealth, the old feudal landowner structures were threatened with the rise in prominence of a new, 'middle class'. Emma's distaste of the Coles stems from their recently acquired wealth; 'They ... by this time were, in fortune and style of living, second only to the family at Hartfield. ... the regular and best families Emma could hardly suppose they would presume to invite – neither Donwell, nor Hartfield, nor Randalls' (Ch. 25, p. 156).

However it is chiefly Emma who appears to cling onto ancient established ideas of social hierarchy – when it suits her. Mr Weston marries a 'portionless' governess (Ch. 2, p. 13); Emma raises no objections to this, and fiercely defends the slight proffered by Mrs Elton; 'I was rather astonished to find her so vary lady-like! But she is really quite the gentlewoman' (Ch. 32, p. 208). She sees nothing wrong with Harriet marrying either Mr Elton or Frank Churchill, but reacts in shock to the same level of inequality when it involves Mr Knightley: 'Such an elevation on her side! Such a debasement on his!' (Ch. 47, pp. 312–13).

Harriet's illegitimacy is a societal hurdle not to be ignored; except by Emma, who does so purely for her own fancy. Mr Knightley, ever the voice of reason, is sensible to this. Emma may be right in assuming that, should Harriet prove to be the daughter of a gentleman, some money and a good marriage combined with her pretty face may in part remove some of the problem of her tainted past. However it would be difficult for her to marry a gentleman; equality of alliance was of paramount importance, as even Mr Elton points out; 'no doubt, there are men who might not object to – Everybody has their level' (Ch. 15, p. 102).

An essential element of the satisfactory conclusion of the novel is this equality of alliance between Emma and Mr Knightley; a uniting of equal fortune, landownership and social status as well as love. Marriages still retained an element of business arrangement among the landed classes, therefore the audience for this novel would highly approve a match such as this for Emma. *Emma* is arguably a work of social satire rather than the social realism adopted by later writers such as Dickens and Mrs Gaskell.

Because the narrative point of view is commanded by Emma, who is completely immersed in her own world, the reality of poverty is glossed over. Emma's inherent snobbery leads to a complete lack of awareness of the needs of those less fortunate than herself. Although 'the poor' exist in Emma's world, they are referred to obliquely in one brief reference in Chapter 10 of the first volume. Emma's visit to a poor family is merely an occasion to exhibit her more altruistic side – albeit fleeting and thus inherently satirical. Austen describes her kindness and sensitivity, but there is no real picture painted of the reality of this facet of society. The event is glossed over without any detail. The many workers and cottagers of Hartfield, Donwell Abbey and Randalls, as well as poor villagers of Hartfield, are never mentioned.

 CHECK THE NET
Search the internet for information on other Victorian novelists and social commentators.

RELATIONSHIPS

As *Emma* is essentially a novel of social manners and the interplay of relations within a microcosm of eighteenth-century English society, the relationships between characters form the essence of plot, structure and narrative. Jane Austen herself was primarily concerned with family relations in her own life, taking pride and joy from the bonds of affection between siblings, parents, nieces and nephews. Thus within her work it is the relationships between the characters which engage and maintain interest. These relationships can be categorised under the following headings: romantic, familial, friendship.

ROMANTIC RELATIONSHIPS

Romance, or the idea of romance, is a driving force in *Emma*. The novel is classed as a 'romantic' work, that is, one primarily concerned with the pursuit of, and satisfactory conclusion of, settled and appropriate romantic partnerships. The comedy of the work, however, derives its chief force from the disparity between actual and perceived partnerships. Although the reader is drawn to make conclusions as to the suitability of certain attachments, notably those between Emma and Mr Knightley, Jane Fairfax and

Romantic relationships continued

Frank Churchill, Harriet Smith and Robert Martin, the course of the novel is steered through a series of 'mis-matched' possibilities before the eventual goal is reached. Furthermore, this novel, as a comedy of social manners, implies that the definition of a 'satisfactory partnership' is between couples of equal social and financial status. However, Austen clearly approves of 'love' matches also: Miss Taylor's marriage to Mr Weston has no such suitability of social status and yet is applauded as the marriage of true minds. What Miss Taylor lacks in financial independence or family status she makes up for in personal integrity and worth. Similarly, the marriage of Jane Fairfax and Frank Churchill, hindered from the outset by social constraints as to inequality of position and wealth is celebrated at the end of the novel as a match of true love.

QUESTION
Examine the relationships of the characters in the novel and discuss who ultimately benefits; those who marry for love, or those who marry for social status?

It is Emma's own overriding concern with social suitability of alliance which dictates the narrative thrust of the plot and the humour. She is a victim of her own snobbery, and the reader observes with mounting **irony** as she attempts to force a series of imaginary partnerships into reality whilst at the same time completely ignoring her own heart. Her misguided attempts to make a match between Harriet and Mr Elton, and then Frank Churchill, are doomed to failure because of forces stronger than her own: namely love and sense of social standing. Mr Elton, ever the social climber, is far more concerned with making a 'good match' than with the influence of a pretty face. When his attempts to ensnare Emma fail so disastrously, he speedily makes a match with a lady of wealth and is immensely satisfied with himself in the process. Although Mrs Elton has no redeeming features in terms of grace, sense or humility, she at least is an heiress. This couple suit each other perfectly: both are enormous snobs and like to brag of their wealthy connections. Harriet provides her own barriers to the satisfactory conclusion of Emma's plans for her: she is, and has always been, in love with Robert Martin. Although she is temporarily swayed by her sense of Emma's superior judgement, her own feelings eventually lead to a happy conclusion for her.

Emma's idea of love changes and develops throughout the novel as she grows in maturity and self-knowledge. From being obsessed with 'fancy' or idealised romance (such as her own fascination with

Frank Churchill before she has even met him), she learns through experience the meaning and importance of real romantic love. Her eventual realisation of what this means is delayed until she experiences such feelings at first hand. Her eventual empathy with Harriet's feelings for Robert Martin, and Frank's for Jane Fairfax, is a direct result of her own growth into a woman deeply in love, rather than a girl who assumes that 'love' is merely a convenient glue to stick two desirable partners together.

FAMILIAL RELATIONSHIPS

Emma's sense of duty and love for her father are her great redeeming features throughout the novel. Even at her most desperate and miserable, she is eager to sacrifice her own comfort and care to making sure Mr Woodhouse is kept comfortable and entertained. She is more than a dutiful daughter; she never questions or complains about the need to ensure her father's comfort above her own. This facet of Emma's personality is the more striking given the demanding and almost insufferable nature of this gentleman's character. When at her most downcast after Mr Knightley's condemnation of her behaviour at the Box Hill party, she determines never to be criticised as a daughter lacking in duty, and concentrates upon ensuring her father's contentment. Mr Woodhouse is accorded the respect and thought due to his seniority, his status in this society and his gentle personality. Although his character appears to be one designed to inspire intense irritation, family and friends defer to his comfort at all times. In this world, duty and respect for age and status are of paramount importance. Emma is not alone in her respectful care towards her father: Isabella, Mrs Weston and chiefly Mr Knightley all make great sacrifices to ensure his comfort.

Similarly, Jane Fairfax endures the prattling of her aunt and the cloistered habitation of her grandmother's home without complaint. She is applauded for her sensitivity to the feelings and welfare of her family in the same way as Emma, and ironically only Emma acknowledges the stress this must put Jane under. She empathises with Jane's position in spite of not recognising that she makes the same kind of sacrifices herself.

CHECK THE BOOK

Weak fathers are common in Austen's novels: Mr Bennet in *Pride and Prejudice* (1813), and Sir Walter Elliot in *Persuasion* (1818) are such examples.

FRIENDSHIP

There are several bonds of friendship in *Emma*. The strong bond of care that exists between Emma and Mrs Weston is not hampered by the latter's marriage and removal to Randalls. Their close bond has been forged through years of constant contact and mutual regard. Their companionable friendship is one of the greatest in the novel, and a striking contrast to that between Emma and Harriet. Obviously it is the disparity of basic sense and intelligence which marks the disparity in the two friendships, notwithstanding all Emma's efforts to the contrary. Harriet is never more than a distraction for her to fill the days following Miss Taylor's marriage.

Jane Fairfax is a more suitable friend for Emma. They have a great deal in common in terms of age, intelligence, family circumstances and accomplishments. It is Emma's jealousy of Jane that impedes a friendship which to everyone around them appears natural and immensely desirable. Only Mr Knightley recognises the inhibiting factor and condemns Emma for her small-mindedness. Only once Emma has undertaken her journey into maturity can the two women meet without restraint, admit their previous coolness and resolve to be friends.

Emma's friendship with Mr Knightley is easy, comfortable and without restraint. They have known each other since Emma's birth and are connected through sibling marriage as well as through being neighbours and family friends. The transition from friendship to love is a relatively easy one and, once the romantic and tender passages which mark the exchange of their declarations of love have been passed through, they return easily to their former teasing banter and comfortable communion with each other. There is no pretence and affectation in this friendship: Mr Knightley knows Emma better than anyone, even herself. It is only with him that she feels free, and it is his censorship which most hurts.

THE POSITION OF WOMEN

During the **Augustan** period the position of women in society was largely dictated by strict codes of expectation. Primarily, women of Emma's rank, that is, the 'genteel' precursors to the middle classes, were constrained by society's expectation to make a match which

CHECK THE NET

Search the internet for early-nineteenth-century feminist writing, in particular the work of Mary Wollstonecraft.

would ensure their respectability and financial comfort. Marriage was as much a business as a matter of the heart.

The parent of a daughter would be concerned with making a suitable match for that daughter and providing the necessary dowry package to enhance the desirability of their child. The path for sons was similarly cast in social stone: eldest sons inherited land, any titles, familial responsibilities and the house or business. Second sons were encouraged to engage in a living as a vicar, and third and subsequent boys usually took up careers in the army or navy as officers. It was not necessary to think in terms of career choices for female children: they would be seen as marriageable propositions primarily. Although Jane Austen eschewed the idea of a loveless marriage, writing to her niece Fanny that 'Anything is to be preferred or endured rather than marrying without affection', many women of her era disagreed with this view and valued financial and social security higher than love.

Women without sufficient financial backing from their families had limited choices. Miss Taylor's position in the Woodhouse household is very unusual: to be kept on as a member of the family after the duty of care to children has ceased is a romantic, idealised view of the role of governess. Jane Fairfax is typical of the breed of young girls brought up to be skilled in the pursuits of a gentlewoman but without the means to make her a marriageable proposition for a man of fortune. Her 'fate' as governess was one familiar to the contemporary readership; Charlotte Brontë and her sisters were placed in similar positions and Charlotte particularly wrote with poignancy in *Jane Eyre* of the enforced servitude and humiliation of the role. Although unattractive as a life-choice, society frowned upon women of genteel breeding supporting themselves by other means such as shop-work, nursing or the stage. Thus it is that Jane is spared this fate by becoming the wife of Frank Churchill, although he has to wait for his aunt to die before he can declare the engagement openly and receive permission from his, less condescending, uncle.

Jane is very lucky, and her happy fate can be seen as a flight of fancy on Jane Austen's part. Although men were permitted to make matches with women without financial and social security if they

> **CONTEXT**
> Propriety and social niceties pervaded every aspect of life; notice how even the order of dancers at the ball is governed by social codes.

were pretty and accomplished, the view espoused by Mr Knightley was more familiar: 'Men of family would not be very fond of connecting themselves with a girl of such obscurity…' (Ch. 8, p. 50). It is Emma's refusal to acknowledge society's codes of expectation which cause so much trouble for her. Mr Knightley's valiant efforts to warn her against setting Harriet up in a match with Mr Elton are wasted because Emma believes that the grace and beauty of her friend will outweigh any concern over the fact that she is illegitimate. Emma is proved wrong: Harriet is lucky to make the match with Robert Martin, the warning offered to him by Mr Knightley: 'My only scruple in advising the match was on his account, as being beneath his deserts, and a bad connexion for him.'

To marry 'well' and proceed to have lots of babies was the respectable course of action for a young lady of gentle breeding. Isabella does just this: she already has five children and is in all respects the dutiful wife and mother. Mrs Weston appears to be following the same course. Emma sees no attraction in this life choice, and positively rails against the desirability of becoming a wife: 'I have none of the usual inducements of women to marry… fortune I do not want; employment I do not want; consequence I do not want' (Ch. 10, pp. 66–7). However, she has not yet experienced love, and recognises this as the only possible reason for marrying relevant to herself.

CHECK THE BOOK

Feminist interpretations of key Austen novels can be found in *Jane Austen and Discourses of Feminism,* ed. Devoney Looser (1995).

Feminist criticism of Austen argues that her female characters are far from typical of the contemporary world. Real women faced more difficult choices and far less attractive fates than Austen's heroines, who almost without exception find a satisfactory fate: a 'happy ending'. However, Austen writes romantic novels and regardless of the social reality of the work, the structure and focus of the genre demands such satisfactory conclusions.

RIDDLES AND GAMES

The theme of playing games, secrets and riddles courses through the entire novel. Emma plays games with the lives and loves of others for her own amusement; only to suffer the poetic justice of, firstly, being used in someone else's own game, and finally becoming primary victim of her own game playing.

As noted by Fiona Stafford in her preface to the 1996 Penguin edition of the text, 'the text is filled with episodes in which the central characters blush, colour, glow or turn red.' The novel is dominated by secrets and hidden meanings; the overall irony stemming from Emma, as central character, believing herself fully 'in the secret' (Ch. 47, p. 312) when in fact she is always completely oblivious to the reality around her.

The message from the novel is that game playing leads to unhappiness. Mr Knightley refuses to play the secrets game; he very early on makes it clear to Emma that he can see through her games and warns her that nothing good will come from it. He guesses at the plot for Harriet to marry Mr Elton, he sees through the game played by Frank Churchill, and condemns both Emma and Frank for their double-dealing; 'does not everything serve to prove more and more the beauty of truth and sincerity in all our dealings with each other?' (Ch. 51, p. 337).

This major theme is reinforced through the imagery of the riddle episode where Mr Elton's meaning, so clear and apparent to everyone else, is completely mistaken by Emma and Harriet. Harriet has the influence of Emma to blame, (as well as her own inherent dullness) but Emma's only excuse is her inability to see what is right under her nose except when it suits her. The game image is repeated in chapter 41, when Emma encourages the word game between Frank and Jane; literally this time not seeing what is under her very nose. The episode at Box Hill is the most painful reminder that playing games leads to pain; Emma's hurtful remarks to Miss Bates immediately stop the game invented by Frank to distract attention from his argument with Jane Fairfax. Even Mrs Elton disapproves of this game; 'I am not at all fond of the sort of thing... I really must be allowed to judge when to speak and when to hold my tongue' (Ch. 51, p. 337). Of course, her objection clearly arises from the idea that Emma is to be made the centre of attention of this game, as Mr Knightley acidly observes; 'This explains the sort of clever thing that is wanted.'

Mr Knightley rightly disapproves of Emma's indolence. Firstly, she makes little good use of her time; 'she will never submit to any thing requiring industry and patience, and a subjection of the fancy to the

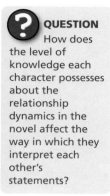

QUESTION
How does the level of knowledge each character possesses about the relationship dynamics in the novel affect the way in which they interpret each other's statements?

understanding' (Ch. 5, p. 29). She has noone but herself to blame for the negative comparison between herself and Jane Fairfax in terms of relative accomplishment. Secondly, and far more dangerously, Emma's natural boredom leads her into all manner of mischief. Like a child, she spends her time playing games rather than working to improve herself.

The game is finally over when all the major characters have had their secrets revealed, and happiness results. The narrator retreats into reported dialogue and screened conversation in these latter stages, allowing the reader to imagine for themselves, for example, the nature and language of the proposal between Harriet and Robert, or Emma's acceptance of Mr Knightley. Thus the integrity of the reader is judged far more trustworthy than the words of the characters. The letter from Frank Churchill is allowed to dominate a whole chapter; standing testament to the high value placed upon complete clarity and honesty. It is important that he lays the mystery completely open, and equally important that this letter is laid open for public scrutiny.

STRUCTURE

Much as the narrative technique of characterisation allows the reader to observe, and understand, the central character more fully, the plot narrative similarly weaves itself around the heroine with her as focus.

Volume I introduces the major characters to the reader. The significant features of the central character's personality are stated, then immediately clarified through observation of her actions. Thus, Emma's indolent nature, desire to play games, arrogant snobbery and belief that she is always right are laid open in Chapter 1 (albeit far more subtly) and then exemplified in her behaviour during that volume. Her indolence is shown in her filling her days with mindless activity; 'It was much easier to chat than to study; much pleasanter to let her imagination range and work at Harriet's fortune, than to be labouring to enlarge her comprehension or exercise it on sober facts' (Ch. 9, p. 54). Game playing and snobbery are both highlighted in her belief that Harriet, now her personal friend, could only be the daughter of a gentleman and as such it is her duty to find a gentleman for her to marry.

The effects of her nature are turned on herself by the end of Volume I as a hilarious result of her intrigue and game playing. The tone of the first volume is cheerful, with no significant lasting negative consequences. Emma redeems herself through evidence of a greater self-understanding, but the reader is prepared for further, possibly more serious, evidence of the effects of these character traits.

Volume II introduces the secondary characters whose presence will dominate the course of the plot development. Frank Churchill and Jane Fairfax arrive on the scene, and preside over this volume, with Emma as unwitting pawn in their own, separately created intrigue. Interestingly, as the plot pursues its natural course towards crisis, the central character is undergoing changes and developments of her own which will aid her when the crisis hits.

The final volume contains the crisis; the result of all the game-playing. However, the crisis is able to be resolved due to the central character's developing maturity and increased self-understanding. Her growth into knowledge is the key to her being finally rewarded with a happy ending rather than the punishment she fears. Emma has to deserve her happiness, and the reader can only feel that sense of **catharsis** if convinced that she has learned from her mistakes and will be a better person in future.

NARRATIVE TECHNIQUES

POINT OF VIEW

The favoured narrative stance adopted by Austen is that of **omniscient narrator**. She narrates in the third person, principally observing the action and development of plot from the point of view of the central character and privy to her thoughts and feelings alone. The omniscient narrator is aware of all, but concentrates her attention upon one main character.

Use of this stance allows a great deal of observational humour, principally through the **ironic** distance it creates. Readers observe through the narrator's unclouded presentation, the reality placed before them without prejudicial narrative commentary. Thus in Chapter 6, the narrator merely has to report Mr Elton's words and behaviour for the reader to see clearly what Emma does not; that his 'raptures' are not intended for Harriet at all.

The narrator seldom steps away from Emma's point of view – vital for the ironic humour to be maintained. Occasionally the reporting of Emma's thoughts allows moments of high ironic comedy, for example during her shock and outrage following Mr Elton's hysterical outburst: 'How could she have been so deceived!' (Ch. 16, p. 103).

IRONIC OBSERVATION

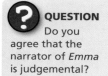

QUESTION
Do you agree that the narrator of *Emma* is judgemental?

Occasionally Austen treats the reader to a moment of delightfully cutting wit, apparently in spite of the desire to remain aloof and retain a judicial courtesy towards her characters. For example, there is an irresistibly disparaging remark made about Mrs Elton: 'Mr Knightley seemed to be trying not to smile; and succeeded without difficulty, upon Mrs Elton's beginning to talk to him' (Ch. 36, p. 236). In the main, however, the reader is merely offered the information and invited to form their own judgements without the interference of narrative commentary or opinion. When Harriet gushes in her customary manner over Emma's friendship, the narrator simply informs us that this 'made Emma feel that she had never loved Harriet so well, not valued her affection so highly before' (Ch. 31, p. 202). Another pointed observation is made in Chapter 10 when Emma muses over the permanent effect on her made by her charitable visit to her impoverished neighbours, which speedily disappears upon sighting Mr Elton.

IRONY OF SITUATION

The novel as a whole is a study in irony in its truest sense; that of difference between actual and perceived meaning. There is irony in Emma's belief that she is the centre of everyone's intrigues and secrets, when in fact she is blind even to her own feelings for Mr Knightley. Her abhorrence of Mrs Elton is remarkable in that the very qualities so disliked by Emma are mere extensions of similar arrogance in herself.

DIRECT SPEECH

The use of free indirect style allows frequent use of direct speech. This technique frees the characters from the constraints of the narrative stance to behave and speak as they feel, and allows the reader to judge them more freely. The essence of Miss Bates is summarised in her first passage of direct speech; 'Oh! Here it is. I was sure it could not be far off; but I had put my huswife upon it, you see, without being aware, and so it was quite hid, but I had it in my hand so very lately that I was almost sure it must be on the table...' (Ch. 19, p. 117).

The style favoured by Austen is without dramatic embellishment or melodrama; in fact, she **satirises** such writing in an earlier work, *Northanger Abbey*. The tone is simple and direct, with actions, situations and speech reported clearly. Developments in such stylistic features would later come to be referred to as psychological **realism**, although Austen's work pre-dates such comparative analysis of novel form.

Mr Knightley makes one observation on Emma's skill at painting, sharply contrasted with Mr Elton's verbose, eloquent praise – he simply remarks; 'you have made her too tall, Emma' (Ch. 6, p. 37). Using direct speech for this statement emphasises the simplicity and direct honesty which **epitomises** his character. In Chapter 15, Austen uses direct speech to mark an oasis of calm and common sense amidst the confusion, thereby clearly delineating her preference for such behaviour;

> Mr Knightley and Emma settled it in a few brief sentences: thus
>
> 'Your father will not be easy; why do not you go?'
>
> 'I am ready, if the others are.'
>
> 'Shall I ring the bell?'
>
> 'Yes, do.'

In Chapter 38 Ch. 15, p. 99 the use of impressionistic dialogue allows the reader to experience the 'hum' of light chatter from the guests at the ball, emphasising the triviality of their conversation.

CHECK THE BOOK

In *Emma* Austen tricks her characters and the reader into a number of wrong interpretations of events; on rereading we can see that all the clues were there for the sharp-eyed. *Pride and Prejudice* (1813) to a lesser degree also plays this trick on the reader.

PART FOUR

CRITICAL HISTORY

EARLY CRITICAL RECEPTION

As early as the year of its appearance, Emma has been criticised for its lack of action and event. When one considers the historical position of the novel and the fact that the plot is contemporary to the composition, it is more remarkable that external events have very little effect on the thrust of the plot. The novel was completed in the year of the Battle of Waterloo itself.

However, other notable critics, most importantly Sir Walter Scott himself, advocated the very antithesis to this argument. In *The Quarterly Review* of 1815, he admired 'the knowledge of the world, and the peculiar tact with which she presents characters that the reader cannot fail to recognise.' The **dichotomy** between the varied interpretations of Austen's art, and the perceived responsibility of an author to represent the voice and mind of the nation, persists into criticism today.

WOMEN WRITING AND FEMINIST CRITICISM

As Ellen Moers, in her essay entitled 'Literary Women' (1978) argues, Austen inhabited a fundamentally female world and established herself as a female writer. Women writers with established crucial reputations were in the minority in the eighteenth century, and Austen herself admitted to being ' the most unlearned and uninformed female who ever dared to be an authoress'. Whilst male contemporaries had each other and their own historical heritage from which to draw, Austen's female contemporaries ranged in reputation between 'excellent, fair and wretched'. Women did not partake of the camaraderie adopted by their male counterparts, school and university were the domains of the man, and many male writers drew benefit from collaboration with their colleagues with whom they found easy proximity.

The danger with much **feminist** literary criticism is that it has a tendency to express, or search for, polarity of viewpoint in its need to justify the essential argument that women are marginalised, shackled, dominated and oppressed by male society. Within the spectrum of criticism labelled 'feminist', there is a wide range of viewpoints however.

Virginia Woolf argues in *A Room of One's Own* (1929) that the very act of writing, of baring one's soul for the edification and/or motivation of one's readership, demands a pronounced level of confidence and innate sense of self. Such self-confidence is more common in the male for whom society is structured to develop and enhance confidence. How much more difficult for women who, she argues, have historically been enchained and dominated by society's expectations. Gilbert and Gubar in their famous essay on female writers, 'The Madwoman in the Attic' (1979), further claim that patriarchal dominance of literature has forced women to find more subversive methods to achieve their aims. They quote Anne Elliot's **ironic** comment that 'men have every advantage of us in telling their story. Education has been theirs in so much higher a degree'. Feminist interpretation of the work of Austen and her female contemporaries argues that the novel was the ideal form for women of the eighteenth century to begin to explore and celebrate their own femininity, whilst relinquishing the ties of a male-dominated society. She states that the novel arose as a direct result of women's need to find a form with which to reconstruct themselves in a changing society. Although her study is primarily concerned with the causality of the female 'hysteric' in work by the Brontë sisters – particularly Cathy in *Wuthering Heights* and Bertha in *Jane Eyre*, there are correlations between this viewpoint and how Jane Austen presents her women characters. Apart from Emma, all Austen's heroines are to a certain extent dependent upon others. They are clear representations of the dependent nature of the role of women in eighteenth-century society; although not manifesting the oppression of the working class, they lack the independence and power of men. Emma is the only heroine freed from financial and familial dependency.

CHECK THE BOOK
See **Further reading** for some suggestions of titles offering detailed critical analysis of *Emma*.

HISTORICIST CRITICISM

There is a range of critical theories under this heading, all of which share the aim of contextualising the particular author within his or her own socio-historical framework. For example, a Marxist critical interpretation of Jane Austen's work would argue that there is little evidence of awareness of a social conscience in her novels: the working classes exist but are ignored by the world she inhabits. The quintessentially 'genteel', landed population of *Emma* and other novels presents a stratum of society built upon the labour and oppression of the working class, and Marxist theory would focus upon this and the notable absence of reference to the rise of Industrial England. Warren Roberts, in *Jane Austen and the French Revolution* (1995), clearly demonstrates this aspect of criticism in the exploration of the European historical context of Austen's work.

RECENT CRITICISM

The scholar Lord David Cecil wrote of Austen in his work *Poets and Storytellers* of 1949; 'Jane Austen's range of character is very large. She painted on such a narrow canvas that people have not always realised this. But a wide canvas does not necessarily mean a wide range... *Emma* is universal just because it is narrow; because it confines itself to the range of Jane Austen's profoundest vision.'

CHECK THE NET
Search the Internet for information on Arnold Kettle's critiques of Austen.

Other critics and writers have commented on the lucidity of her style, her snobbery and obsession with trivia, the limited range of vision, her astute vision of the inner psyche. This polarity of opinion is summarised delightfully by the writer Quentin Bell, who remembers a disagreement with a fellow writer over the character of Emma:

> Emma he maintained was a very unpleasant character, a desperate snob, callous, conceited and vain....I replied that although she had her faults she did suffer from an unbearably silly father and that she bore his silliness with exemplary patience.

> For a moment he was at a loss, but he was not a man who could easily be put down, and he responded, almost seriously: 'Well, we've only got Jane Austen's word for it.' Which is, I suppose the highest praise that one can give a novelist.

(*Elders and Betters*, 1997)

PART FIVE

BACKGROUND

JANE AUSTEN'S LIFE AND WORKS

Jane Austen was born at her father's rectory at Steventon, a small country village in Hampshire, on 16 December 1775. She was the sixth child and second daughter of reverend George Austen and his wife Cassandra. Her elder sister was named after her mother. Her father was an Anglican clergyman who had been a fellow of St John's College, Oxford. Accompanied by Cassandra, her elder sister and life-long friend, she went to school first at Oxford and then at Reading, but her education was completed at home under the supervision of her father. Her subsequent life was happy yet uneventful; her father was comfortably off and she enjoyed a good relationship with the other members of the family. Her grandfather William had enjoyed a good career as a surgeon and, with financial aid from members of his family, had had his son educated at Oxford. Thus whilst not enjoying the easy prosperity of the landed gentry, the family had a comfortable home and lifestyle.

Jane's parents ran a school for boys alongside the rectory, where her brothers were educated until they were of an age to go to boarding school. There were five brothers, four of them older than Jane and Cassandra. The eldest, James, went to Oxford, like his father, and later succeeded him as Rector of Steventon. The second brother, George, did not live with the family and little is known of him other than the fact that he was victim to a lifelong debilitation from an undiagnosed illness which had a profound effect on him mentally and physically.

Like Frank Churchill, the third brother Edward was adopted by a local wealthy family without children of their own and later inherited the estate of Godmersham Park in Kent. This event was not at all unusual to this era, where it was viewed as extremely advantageous to have a member of one's family taken under the wing of benign prosperity. In return for the fortunes, this arrangement ensured that the family name would live on. The event and its resulting fortunes for Edward proved to be the lifesaver of

 CHECK THE NET

There is a Jane Austen Centre also in Bath: see its website at **http://www. janeausten.co.uk** for all kinds of information about Austen.

his brother George and his sisters in later years, when following the death of their father, they became homeless and reliant on the goodwill of friends and relatives for places to stay. Edward stepped in and offered them a house on his estate at Godmersham; the 'cottage' in the village of Chawton in Hampshire became the Austen's home for the remainder of Jane's life.

CHECK THE BOOK

Two recent biographies are David Nokes: *Jane Austen* (1997) and Claire Tomalin: *Jane Austen: A Life* (1997).

The fourth brother Henry was the charmer and favourite of the family – especially for Jane, who was devoted to him all her life. He found it hard to settle on one career, becoming first a captain in the Militia, later a London banker – which brought him great success until his bank crashed and he became a vicar like his father and eldest brother. Edward, now known as 'Knight' after the family who had adopted him, granted Henry the living in a country parish of his estate. The other two brothers, Frank and Charles, both entered the navy at twelve years of age and enjoyed long and successful careers, becoming admirals of the fleet and being distinguished in the Napoleonic Wars.

Jane and her sister Cassandra were devoted to each other all their lives. When Jane was seven, they were sent away to a succession of boarding schools as their parents were engaged daily with the school for boys they ran themselves. Accounts from this period attest to the harshness of this world; both girls were relieved to complete their formal education four years later and return home permanently. Their father, an educated man himself, continued their education sensibly; French, Italian, classical reading and piano were studied. Jane's education followed a pattern considered reasonable and appropriate for young ladies, clearly much the same as that followed by Emma under the benign dictates of Miss Taylor. Among her reading Austen cited Fanny Burney, Henry Fielding, Laurence Sterne and Samuel Richardson as great favourites. She also admired the style of Samuel Johnson, and the poetry of Sir Walter Scott and George Crabbe.

When Jane was twenty six, her father retired from his parish and took his wife and daughters to live in Bath. Jane was very unhappy to leave her family home and disliked Bath intensely. However, the move afforded a richer slice of society life, and both sisters were launched into the world of balls and visiting previously unknown to them. The sisters spent a great deal of time visiting family and friends, particularly in Kent and Hampshire. It was the country that Jane knew well and the setting for many of her novels.

Whilst in Hampshire, Jane received a proposal from an old friend of the family with a large house and estate. Jane accepted him, but for some reason the next day changed her mind and left with Cassandra immediately for Bath. Cassandra, engaged the while to a naval officer, was still in mourning for his death from fever in the West Indies. It appears that after this time both young women retreated from society, giving up dancing and taking up the characteristics of old maids. The period after her father's death in 1805 was turbulent and unsettled for the family, but once settled at Chawton in 1809, Jane's life became much calmer and happier. She resumed her writing and appeared content in her limited social life, restricting her engagements to visits to her brothers every so often. However early in 1816 she contracted tuberculosis. She died at the age of 41 on 18 July 1817, and her body was buried in Winchester Cathedral.

CHECK THE NET
Explore the Jane Austen information page at **http://www. pemberley.com.**

HER WORKS

From the age of twelve, Austen was a prolific writer. She produced a series of sketches and tales, the most important of which was a mock-serious and deliberately absurd tale entitled *Love and Friendship*; finally published in 1923.

At around twenty years of age she began her first major work; the novel *Lady Susan*, which remained unpublished during her lifetime. She then embarked on *Elinor and Marianne*, which although completed in 1797, when she was twenty-two, was not published until 1811 – under the title of *Sense and Sensibility*. This work was first written as a series of letters but did not find favour amongst publishers and was rewritten before publication. As an advocate of the **epistolary style** of Samuel Richardson as well as a prolific and skilled letter writer herself, Jane was discouraged and disappointed by this rejection but learnt to adapt her style to accommodate the tastes of her publishers and became mistress of the third person narrative technique. Her third work, given the title *First Impressions*, was completed in 1798 and sent by her father to a publisher who refused it. It was later published as *Pride and Prejudice* in 1813. Between 1798 and 1803 she was engaged with

Northanger Abbey which was sold to a publisher in 1803 but did not appear in print until 1818, one year after her death.

There was a pause in literary activity during the years of family upheaval, and it was not until the remove to Chawton when Jane felt happy and settled enough to begin writing again. *Mansfield Park* was published in 1814, *Emma* in 1816 and *Persuasion*, published posthumously in 1818 alongside *Northanger Abbey*. Her last work, *Sandition*, remained unfinished at her death. Thus *Emma* was the fourth novel published in her lifetime although it was her penultimate finished novel.

Jane Austen was not a professional writer and did not enjoy early success. However, she had become a favourite with the Prince Regent, son of George III and later to become King George IV. She was invited by his librarian to dedicate a work to this esteemed patron and did so, albeit reluctantly as she despised the man. Nevertheless, the pragmatist in her paid due accord to the honour bestowed and the first publication of Emma had its dedication page dutifully noted. Austen later wrote a stunning *satirical* response to the Regent's librarian's suggestions for a later novel.

LITERARY PERSPECTIVE

Samuel Richardson has been dubbed the father of the English novel; his *Pamela* was published in 1740 in the **epistolary style** which Austen sought to emulate in the first draft of *Sense and Sensibility*. Alongside Henry Fielding, Tobias Smollet and Laurence Sterne, the novel came into being during this **Age of Reason**. Novelists of this time encouraged moral principles and **realism**. There was little of great literary value published in the latter half of the eighteenth century, and it was only when Austen and Sir Walter Scott began to work and publish that the novel form began to gain prominence. The pair were very different in tone and style; Austen was always a social **satirist** and realist, whilst Scott preferred delving into legend and history, and his heroes were knights and lords of bygone days.

The next really great novelist after Scott – and possibly the greatest in the history of English Literature – was Charles Dickens, who

CHECK THE BOOK

Typical eighteenth-century satirical writing relies on a shared foundation of values in author and audience in order to be comprehensible. Try reading some of Pope's 'Epistle II. To A Lady: Of the Characters of Women' (1735). The poet castigates what he regards as folly of the world from the relative security of a mutually understood 'common sense' in which he assumes his reader participates. Is this true of Jane Austen's irony?

began in 1836 with *The Pickwick Papers*. Dickens' novels live through his characterisation. In his writings, too; there is a strong sociological and humanitarian leaning: Dickens revealed to the reading public some of the horrors of the conditions in which millions of Britain's population lived, and we must therefore regard him as a social reformer as much as a writer of fiction. Four other Victorian novelists took their cue from Dickens – Thackeray, the Bronte sisters, Elizabeth Gaskell and George Eliot. Subsequent major nineteenth-century novelists included Thomas Hardy and Anthony Trollope.

Austen was a great admirer of her predecessors but was writing at a relatively early period for the novel. She greatly admired Fielding and Richardson, adored the common sense and moderation of Dr Johnson, but had particular regard for the technical skill of her contemporary Maria Edgeworth. She also loved the novels of Fanny Burney and Charlotte Smith. Her father had owned an extensive library and she had read widely from being a child. From the critical essays of Joseph Addison and Dr Johnson, Austen found fellow advocates of sound common sense and respect for moderation; characteristics of the **Augustan age** in English Literature. As the title *Sense and Sensibility* suggests, the cultural movement towards **Romanticism** in the latter part of the eighteenth century was less comfortable. She satirised a return to the emotive and melodramatic **gothic** in *Northanger Abbey*.

The upper and middle classes were relatively new to the process and pursuit of reading; there is a natural and obvious correlation between the increase in numbers learning to read and of appropriate reading matter becoming available to them. Furthermore, there was plenty of time available for these sections of society to use for reading, particularly for women who were not allowed to share in many of the leisure pursuits of their menfolk. The breed of women referred to by Ian Watt in *The Rise of the Novel* as 'omnivorous readers' needed fodder with which to be entertained.

A contemporary of Austen, Mary Shelley, published *Frankenstein* in 1818. As a work of philosophical and ideological exploration, it is markedly different from the novels of Jane Austen who was more concerned with exploring and satirising middle-class society. Later

CHECK THE BOOK

Mary Wollstonecraft, the feminist writer, was the mother of Mary Shelley, author of *Frankenstein*.

writers such as Mrs Gaskell, George Eliot and Charles Dickens also took a wider view in their condemnation of the inequality of society.

Like her female successors, Austen was aware of the disapproval attached to women writers and published anonymously; although she never took a male pseudonym as the Brontës (Currer, Ellis and Acton Bell) and Mary Ann Evans (George Eliot) decided to do. However, her anonymity was soon discovered and she enjoyed great critical success in her lifetime. Alongside the Prince Regent, another loyal advocate and admirer of her work was Sir Walter Scott, who recognised the modern realism of Austen's style. However, it was not until around fifty years after her death that her novels began to be recognised for their worth in literary circles. Virginia Woolf was among those notable writers who publicly commended Austen for her deftness and sureness of touch with the central character, and recognised those fledgling touches of the style of psychological realism evident in her later work.

JANE AUSTEN'S WORLD

As a daughter of the eighteenth century, Austen lived a remote and sheltered life in a comparatively remote part of the country where literary and other trends and fashions held sway long after they had been superseded in the big towns. It is not surprising, therefore, to find that her favourite authors were the giants of the eighteenth century, the writers of the **Age of Reason**; the European shift towards philosophical realism elsewhere named The Enlightenment. It is not difficult to see the influence of this careful, conservative, reasonable style espoused by Dr Johnson. In many ways, Mr Knightley **epitomises** these values, representing the Voice of Reason making itself heard above the trivialities and excitements of Emma's circle.

CHECK THE NET
Search the internet for 'Feudal Baronetcy' and the historical precedent for the landed gentry.

Austen's sheltered life gave her food enough for six great novels. In an age when class distinctions were much sharper than they are today, governed by immutable laws of propriety, and when life in rural England appeared less threatened by economic and political changes, her days ran along quietly in the contented world of the country gentry and the upper middle class. However, elsewhere in the country, arguably the greatest period of upheaval was taking place. The Industrial Revolution had begun in the earlier part of that century, changing the economic climate forever and introducing a third, 'middle' class to Britain. These merchants and factory owners enjoyed great prosperity during this period and put paid to the old feudal class system in England forever. Mechanical inventions transformed labour patterns by introducing the notion of factory production with all its dreadful problems of child labour, air pollution, high machine-related mortality and the creation of slum housing as thousands of poor farm-workers swarmed to the growing cities for work. The results of the rise of factory production – creation of cities with the inherent problems of housing, poverty and sickness – became the subject matter of the novels of Mrs Gaskell and Dickens later on in the nineteenth century.

In the North of England, starting around Nottingham, weavers put out of work by mechanical looms were vandalising factories under cover of darkness. In 1813, fourteen of these 'Luddites', as these workers became known, were brutally hanged – this only two years before *Emma* was published.

Advances in technical production and the export and import of materials also facilitated the spread of lucrative colonial activity abroad, and it is not to be forgotten that Britain only passed the Abolition of Slavery Act in 1807, slavery's main centres having been Bristol and Liverpool; slavery was not finally abolished in the West Indies until 1834, and continued in some Latin American countries until the 1880s. The Napoleonic Wars were fought during Austen's lifetime, as was the American War of Independence and the French Revolution.

England observed the political revolutions in America and France but participated in a profound social revolution itself.

CONTEXT

'Colonel' and 'Captain' remind the reader that at the time of writing, Britain was engaged not only in a war with America but also the Napoleonic Wars with France and Spain.

World events	Jane Austen's life	Literary events
		1740 Samuel Richardson, *Pamela*
		1746 Henry Fielding, *The History of Tom Jones*
		1752 Fielding, *Amelia*
		1759 Laurence Sterne, *Tristram Shandy*
1760 George III accedes to British throne		
		1765 Horace Walpole, *The Castle of Otranto*
	1775 Jane Austen born, sixth child of the rector of Steventon, Hampshire	**1778** Fanny Burney, *Evelina*
1780 Britain at war with Holland; anti-Catholic Gordon riots in London		
		1782 Burney, *Cecilia*
1783 William Pitt, aged 24, becomes prime minister	**1783** Jane sent with sister Cassandra to Oxford to be taught by Mrs Cawley	**1783** George Crabbe, *The Village*
1784 American War of Independence ends	**1784** Jane sent to Abbey School near Reading	**1784** Samuel Johnson dies
	1785 Jane returns home	**1785** William Cowper, *The Task*
		1786 William Beckford, *Valtek*
1789 French Revolution begins; Jeremy Bentham expounds theory of Utilitarianism		
1793 France declares war on Great Britain; Louis XVI guillotined; reign of terror	**1793-4** Probably writes Lady Susan	**1794** Mrs Radcliffe, *The Mysteries of Udolpho*
	1795 Writes comic *History of the World*	**1795** Matthew Gregory Lewis, *The Monk*

World events	Jane Austen's life	Literary events
	1795-6 Writes *Elinor and Marianne* (later recast as *Sense and Sensibility*)	
	1797 Writes First Impressions (later recast as *Pride and Prejudice*)	
	1789-9 Writes *Northanger Abbey*	
1798 Irish Rebellion put down		**1798** Wordsworth and Coleridge, *Lyrical Ballards*
1799 British fighting Mahratta Wars in India		
		1800 Maria Edgeworth, *Castle Rackrent*
1801 Act of Union between Britain and Ireland	**1801** Austen family move to Bath	
	1802 Reputed to have had a romance	
	1803 Lover dies; proposal by wealthy Hampshire landowner accepted, but retracted next day	
1804 Napoleon declared Emperor of France	**1804** Begins unfinished novel, *The Watsons*	
1805 Battle of Trafalgar	**1805** Father dies	**1805** Walter Scott, *The Lay of the Last Minstrel*
	1806 Family moves to Southampton	
1807 Slave Trade abolished in Britain		
1808-14 Britain at war with French in Spain and Portugal	**1809** Family moves to Chawton, Hampshire	
1810 George III insane; Goya begins *Disasters of War*		

World events	Jane Austen's life	Literary events
1811 Beginning of Regency; machine-breaking Luddite riots	**1811** *Sense and Sensibility* published; *Mansfield Park* begun	
1812-14 America at war with Britain		**1812** Lord Byron, *Childe Harold's Pilgrimage*
	1814 Begins to write *Emma*	**1814** Walter Scott, *Waverley*
1815 Corn Laws passed; Battle of Waterloo; riots after bad harvest and heavy taxation	**1815** Begins writing *Persuasion*	
	1817 Begins unfinished novel *Sanditon*; dies aged 41	
	1818 *Northanger Abbey* and *Persuasion* published posthumously	**1818** Mary Shelley, *Frankenstein*
		1821 John Keats dies
		1822 Shelley dies
		1847 Charlotte Brontë, *Jane Eyre*

FURTHER READING

Maggie Lane & David Selwyn, *Jane Austen, A Celebration,* Carcanet, 2000

>Further remembrances and thoughts about Austen and her work

James-Edward Austen-Leigh, *A Memoir of Jane Austen,* 1870

>Memoir by her nephew

R. W. Chapman, *Jane Austen's Letters,* OUP, 1932

>Publishes the bulk of Jane Austen's surviving letters

Deirdre Le Faye, *Jane Austen's Letters,* 1995

>A more recent edition of the letters

Christopher Gillie, *Jane Austen,* Preface series, Longman, 1985

>Provides a series of critical essays on the novels with particular attention to *Emma*

David Cecil, *A Portrait of Jane Austen,* Constable, 1978

>A thorough and comprehensive guide to the life and work of the author

B. C. Southam (ed.) *Jane Austen: the Critical Heritage,* Routledge, 1968

>A collection of critical essays, references and comments from the author's lifetime until around 1870

CRITICAL WORK ON *EMMA*:

Arnold Kettle, *Emma,* Hutchinson University Library, 1951

David Lodge, *Jane Austen's 'Emma', a Selection of Critical Essays,* Macmillan (Casebook series), 1968

J.F. Burrows, *Jane Austen's 'Emma',* Methuen, 1969

BIOGRAPHY

Elizabeth Jenkins, *Jane Austen, a Biography,* Macdonald, 1956

Marghanita Laski, *Jane Austen and Her World*, Thames and Hudson, 1969

David Nokes, *Jane Austen. A Life*, Fourth Estate, 1997

Claire Tomalin, *Jane Austen: A Life*, Viking, 1997

OTHER WORKS CITED IN THESE NOTES

Quentin Bell, *Elders and Betters,* Pimlico, 1997

David Cecil, *Poets and Storytellers*, Constable, 1949

Sandra Gilbert and Susan Gubar, *The Madwoman in the Attic*, Yale University Press, 1979

Ellen Moers, *Literary Women*, Women's Press, 1978

Warren Roberts, *Jane Austen and the French Revolution*, Athlone, 1995

Virginia Woolf, *A Room of One's Own*, Hogarth Press, 1929

FILM ADAPTATIONS:

There have been two BBC TV adaptations, one in 1948 and one in 1960.

For feature films, there are four versions:

1972, *Emma* starring Doran Godwin and John Carson

1995, *Clueless* starring Alicia Silverstone and Paul Stephen Rudd

1996, *Emma* starring Gwyneth Paltrow and Jeremy Northam

1996, *Emma* starring Kate Beckinsale and Mark Strong

INTERNET INFORMATION:

There are various web sites devoted to the study and discussion of Jane Austen and her work. Although few focus upon literary criticism, there is plenty of information to be found about the world of Jane Austen.

LITERARY TERMS

Age of Reason a loose term for the Restoration and Augustan age (From 1660–1745) and for the eighteenth century in general, when the ideal of reason dominated intellectual activity

Augustan age originally meaning the age of Emperor Augustus (27BC–AD14), it has come to refer to the brilliant literary movement in imitation of this which flourished in the first half of the eighteenth century, particularly during the reign of Queen Anne (1702–14). Writers such as Addison, Steele, Pope and Swift admired Roman writers and attempted to adopt their sense of decorum and balance, their elegant wit, patriotism and concern for society and for good taste

catharsis a term devised by Aristotle to explain the effect of tragic drama on an audience: the purging or purification of emotions through the evocation of pity and fear

closure the feeling of completeness and finality achieved by the ending of some literary works; especially associated with the classic realist texts of the nineteenth century

dichotomy division into two distinct parts

dramatic irony when the audience or reader knows more than the characters, occasioning many ironies

epistolary style written in the form of a series of letters

epitomise encapsulate the meaning of in a short and pithy way

feminist criticism one of the main tenets of feminist thought is that male ways of perceiving and ordering are inscribed into the prevailing ideology of society and into language itself. Literature is seen as a focus for the preconceptions and prejudices that can be discovered by feminist analysis. Feminist critics are therefore very conscious of the role that gender may have in the creation of a literary work and the reader's response to it

gothic in the eighteenth century used to describe any work of art which appeared fantastic or eerie

historicism the idea that all system of thought must be seen within an historical perspective; traditional historicist critics attempt to place a literary work within its historical context

imagery the use of figurative language to evoke sense-impressions

irony a form of sarcasm. Saying one thing and meaning another. A norm is established and then subverted

LITERARY TERMS

Marxist criticism criticism which considers literature in relation to its capacity to reflect the struggle between the classes, and the economic conditions which, according to Karl Marx and Friedrich Engels, lie at the basis of man's intellectual and social evolution

metaphor one thing is described in terms of its resemblance to another, without using 'like' or 'as': it becomes the other object

omniscient narrator a storyteller who has a god-like knowledge of events and of thoughts and feelings in the minds of characters

pathetic fallacy used to describe the habit of a writer of assuming an equation between their own mood and the world about them, for example, a feeling of sadness echoed in grey skies

poetic justice the idea that literature should always depict a world in which virtue and vice are eventually rewarded and punished appropriately

realism, realist a realist author represent the world as it is rather than as it should be, using description rather than invention; observes and documents everyday life in straightforward prose, draws on characters from all levels of society, but often from the lowest classes, represents their speech and manners accurately. Realism became the dominant form of literature in the nineteenth century

reportage a journalist's style of reporting

Romantic period covers a range of tendencies in literature, art and culture that emerged at the end of the eighteenth century and dominated the early years of the nineteenth. Generally, it involved a movement away from the sceptical, rational, formal culture of the eighteenth century and aimed to liberate the creative imagination. The Romantics rejected the limitations of form and precedent and saw themselves as individuals who could express themselves according to their imagination. They explored everything that was felt to be mysterious, remote, unnerving, and assumed the mantle of prophets; the poet became a special kind of person, set apart from the other people. They saw nature as unmodified by humanity, inherently dazzling and elevating; and believe that humanity should learn from nature personified as 'Nature'. Byron, with his brooding, dark good looks, came to epitomise the Romantic hero

satire a work of literature in which folly, evil or topical issues are held up to scorn through ridicule or irony or exaggeration. In Jane Austen's case it is the middle class which is the butt of her satire

stream of consciousness a common narrative technique in modern literature, in which the author attempts to convey all the contents of a character's mind in relation to the stream of experience as it passes by, in a random kind of way

AUTHOR OF THESE NOTES

Sarah Darragh is currently an English examiner for one of the largest examination bodies, and Head of English at a large comprehensive school in Sheffield. She is also author of several York Notes.

Maya Angelou
I Know Why the Caged Bird Sings

Jane Austen
Pride and Prejudice

Alan Ayckbourn
Absent Friends

Elizabeth Barrett Browning
Selected Poems

Robert Bolt
A Man for All Seasons

Harold Brighouse
Hobson's Choice

Charlotte Brontë
Jane Eyre

Emily Brontë
Wuthering Heights

Shelagh Delaney
A Taste of Honey

Charles Dickens
David Copperfield
Great Expectations
Hard Times
Oliver Twist

Roddy Doyle
Paddy Clarke Ha Ha Ha

George Eliot
Silas Marner
The Mill on the Floss

Anne Frank
The Diary of a Young Girl

William Golding
Lord of the Flies

Oliver Goldsmith
She Stoops to Conquer

Willis Hall
The Long and the Short and the Tall

Thomas Hardy
Far from the Madding Crowd
The Mayor of Casterbridge
Tess of the d'Urbervilles
The Withered Arm and other Wessex Tales

L.P. Hartley
The Go-Between

Seamus Heaney
Selected Poems

Susan Hill
I'm the King of the Castle

Barry Hines
A Kestrel for a Knave

Louise Lawrence
Children of the Dust

Harper Lee
To Kill a Mockingbird

Laurie Lee
Cider with Rosie

Arthur Miller
The Crucible
A View from the Bridge

Robert O'Brien
Z for Zachariah

Frank O'Connor
My Oedipus Complex and Other Stories

George Orwell
Animal Farm

J.B. Priestley
An Inspector Calls
When We Are Married

Willy Russell
Educating Rita
Our Day Out

J.D. Salinger
The Catcher in the Rye

William Shakespeare
Henry IV Part I
Henry V
Julius Caesar
Macbeth
The Merchant of Venice
A Midsummer Night's Dream
Much Ado About Nothing
Romeo and Juliet
The Tempest
Twelfth Night

George Bernard Shaw
Pygmalion

Mary Shelley
Frankenstein

R.C. Sherriff
Journey's End

Rukshana Smith
Salt on the snow

John Steinbeck
Of Mice and Men

Robert Louis Stevenson
Dr Jekyll and Mr Hyde

Jonathan Swift
Gulliver's Travels

Robert Swindells
Daz 4 Zoe

Mildred D. Taylor
Roll of Thunder, Hear My Cry

Mark Twain
Huckleberry Finn

James Watson
Talking in Whispers

Edith Wharton
Ethan Frome

William Wordsworth
Selected Poems

A Choice of Poets

Mystery Stories of the Nineteenth Century including The Signalman

Nineteenth Century Short Stories

Poetry of the First World War

Six Women Poets

For the AQA Anthology:

Duffy and Armitage & Pre-1914 Poetry

Heaney and Clarke & Pre-1914 Poetry

Poems from Different Cultures